FOOTPATHS OF BRITAIN
SOUTH

p

Created and produced by
The Bridgewater Book Company Ltd,
Lewes, East Sussex

ISBN: 1-40540-506-6

Printed in China

www.walkingworld.com

Visit the Walkingworld website at
www.walkingworld.com

All the walks in this book are available in more
detailed form on the Walkingworld website.
The route instructions have photographs at key
decision points to help you to navigate, and
each walk comes with an Ordnance Survey®
map. Simply print them out on A4 paper
and you are ready to go! A modest annual
subscription gives you access to over 1,400
walks, all in this easy-to-follow format. If you
wish, you can purchase individual walks for a
small fee.

Next to every walk in this book you will see
a Walk ID. You can enter this ID number on
Walkingworld's 'Find a Walk' page and you will
be taken straight to the details of that walk.

CONTENTS

Introduction

Britain is a fabulous place to walk. We are blessed with a varied and beautiful landscape, a dense network of public footpaths and places of historical interest at every corner. Add to all this the many thousands of well-placed pubs, tea shops and visitor attractions, and it's easy to see why walking is a treasured pastime for millions of people.

Walking is the perfect way to keep fit and healthy. It is good for your heart, muscles and body generally, without making the extreme demands of many sports. For most walkers, however, the health benefits are secondary. We walk for the sheer pleasure of it – being able to breathe in the fresh air, enjoy the company of our friends and 'get away from it all'.

Equipment

If you take up walking as a hobby, it is quite possible to spend a fortune on specialist outdoor kit. But you really don't need to. Just invest in a few inexpensive basics and you'll be ready to enjoy any of the walks in this book.

For footwear, boots are definitely best as they provide you with ankle support and protection from the inevitable mud, nettles and puddles. A light-weight pair should be fine if you have no intention of venturing up big hills or over rugged terrain. If you are not sure what to get, go to a specialist shop and ask for advice. Above all, choose boots that fit well and are comfortable.

Take clothing to deal with any weather that you may encounter. Allow for the 'wind-chill' factor – if your clothes get wet you will feel this cooling effect even more. Carry a small rucksack with a spare top, a hat and waterproofs, just in case. The key is being able to put on and take off layers of clothing at will and so keep an even, comfortable temperature throughout the day.

It's a good idea to carry some food and drink. Walking is exercise and you need to replace the fluid you lose through perspiration. Take a bottle of soft drink or water, and sip it regularly rather than downing it in one go. The occasional chocolate bar, sandwich or biscuit can work wonders when energy levels are flagging.

Walking poles – the modern version of the walking stick – are worth considering. They help you to balance and allow your arms to take some of the strain when going uphill. They also lessen the impact on your knees on downhill slopes. Don't be fooled into thinking that poles are just for the older walker – they are popular with trekkers and mountaineers of all ages.

Finding your way

Most walkers use Ordnance Survey® maps, rightly considered to be among the most accurate, up-to-date and 'walker–friendly' in the world. The 1:50,000 scale Landranger series has long been a favourite of outdoor enthusiasts. Almost all areas of Britain are also covered by the more detailed 1:25,000 scale Explorer and Explorer OL series. These include features such as field boundaries, farm buildings and small streams.

Having a map and compass – and learning how to use them – is vital to being safe in the countryside. Compass and map skills come with practice – there is no substitute for taking them out and having a go. Buy a compass with a transparent base plate and rotating dial; you will find this type in any outdoor shop. Most come with simple instructions – if not, ask in the shop for a guide.

If this all sounds a bit serious, I urge you not to worry too much about getting lost. We have all done it – some of us more often than we care to admit! You are unlikely to come to much harm unless you are on a featureless hilltop or out in very poor weather. If you want to build up your confidence, start with shorter routes through farmland or along the coastline and allow yourself plenty of time.

There are plenty of walks in this book that are perfect for the beginner. You can make navigating even easier by downloading the routes in this book from Walkingworld's website: www.walkingworld.com. These detailed walk instructions feature a photograph at each major decision point, to help you confirm your position and see where to go next.

Another alternative is to join a local walking group

Marsh		Lake/sea
Railway + station		
Dismantled railway		Woods
Route of walk		
A Road		Sand
B Road		Dunes
Footpath		Urban
Track/unclassified road		
Stream		
River		
Large river/estuary		

0   1 km   1 mile

Difficulty Rating

Gentle Stroll   Moderate Walk

Easy Walk   Hill Scramble

Time

Each circle = 1 hour

Half circle = ½ hour

and learn from others. There are hundreds of such groups around the country, with members keen to share their experience and skills.

Enough words. Take the walks in this book as your inspiration. Grab your map and compass, and put on your boots. It's time to go out and walk!

Have fun.

DAVID STEWART *Walkingworld*

▲ Map: Explorer 163
▲ Distance: 5.64 km/3½ miles
▲ Walk ID: 873 Ian Elmes

Difficulty rating

Time

▲ River, Pub, Toilets, Castle, Great Views, Food Shop

Hoo Marina from Lower Upnor via the Saxon Shore Way

This walk begins in the delightful village of Lower Upnor, then follows part of the Saxon Shore Way along the River Medway. The route continues into Hoo, then back across open fields to Lower Upnor.

1 From the car park, turn right towards the Medway Yacht Club. At the gate, bear right and follow the footpath to the end. Drop down to the beach and follow the Saxon Shore Way. Follow the raised footpath at the Wilsonian Sailing Club, then continue along the beach, following the line of the river.

2 When you reach a raised footpath, follow this to the Hoo Ness Yacht Club. Go through the gateway and follow the track ahead, bearing right just before the white gate. Follow this path until you reach a car parking area. Follow the high metal fence, then walk along the road past the Marina Office.

3 Continue straight ahead, along a gravel track then a footpath. Out in the open, bear right, following the 'Saxon Shore' marker post. Walk past the yachts to the end of the path. By the fence, turn right to cross the road and walk between the bus depot and the steel works.

4 Cross the road and follow the footpath left of Whitton Marina, coming out opposite a factory. Turn left along the road. Take the footpath directly ahead of you towards three distant houses. Before you reach the houses, bear left onto another path to the road.

5 Turn left at the main road, then right on the farm track by Church Farm Lodge. Follow the track up the hill. Go through the gate at the top. At the crossroads, go straight on, following the track to an enclosed footpath past some houses.

6 Turn left and follow the road up the hill. At the top, follow the enclosed footpath straight ahead. Ignoring the footpath to the right, carry straight on, following the footpath down towards the river, bearing left at the yellow marker post. At the bottom, follow the road back to the car park.

access information

Lower Upnor lies just off the A228 north of Rochester. The walk starts at the car park.

further information

The village of Lower Upnor is ideal for spending relaxed evenings, with two pubs, great views across to Chatham Historic Dockyard, and a steady stream of yachts going up and down the river. Nearby Upper Upnor also has two pubs and a castle.

A scene of peace and tranquillity is often the reward when taking this riverside walk.

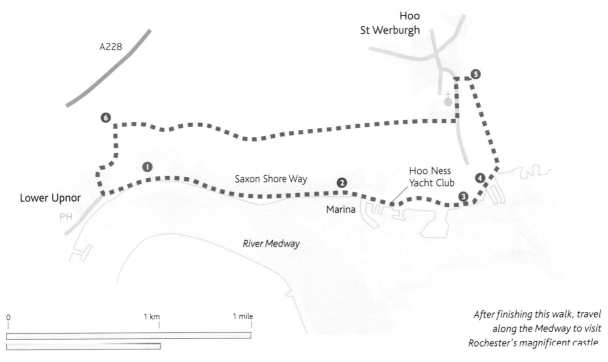

Hoo
St Werburgh

A228

6

Lower Upnor

PH

1

Saxon Shore Way

2

Marina

Hoo Ness
Yacht Club

5

4

3

River Medway

0   1 km   1 mile

*After finishing this walk, travel
along the Medway to visit
Rochester's magnificent castle.*

▲ Map: Explorer 159

▲ Distance: 9.66 km/6 miles

▲ Walk ID: 688 Tony Brotherton

Difficulty rating

Time

▲ Hills, River, Lake, Pub, Toilets, Museum, Church, Wildlife, Birds, Flowers, Great Views

The Kennet & Avon Canal and Padworth Lock from Aldermaston

This circular walk covers a section of the Kennet & Avon Canal and the River Kennet, together with fields, woods and gentle inclines to the south, combining the bustle and colour of canal locks and longboats with quiet rural interludes.

❶ From the car park, cross the road and turn left. Go through a gate to the canal at Aldermaston Wharf. Turn left along the bank and over the bridge at the road. Follow the path to Froudes Bridge. Leave the path, cross the bridge and rejoin the path on the opposite bank.

❷ Follow the canal to the river. Turn right and proceed through the woods to cross Wickham Knights bridge. Turn left along the opposite riverbank. Follow the footpath diversion through the woods to rejoin the river where it meets the canal.

❸ Walk on, then follow an arrow diagonally right across a field. Cross a stream and bear right towards a footbridge leading into a small car park. Cross the A340 and turn left. Take a footpath to the right just before Aldermaston Bridge.

❹ Go through double gates into a poplar copse. At the 'Wasing Estate' sign, follow a right-hand path through the copse to a footbridge and squeeze-stile. Cross three fields over footbridges to a wide track. Turn left. Turn right over the next stile and follow the footpath over a series of stiles. Climb a stile to the road.

❺ Turn left. At the top of the hill, turn left. Follow the footpath to a stile. Bear half-right to another stile. Cross the next field, to descend to a stile into woodland. Follow the path left, then right at a pond, and leave the woods. Before a gate, climb a stile to the left to a fenced strip. At the top, go through the gate. Follow the left-hand meadow boundary. Climb a stile into a lane.

❻ Turn left. After the right bend, turn left through woods. Cross a footbridge over a stream. Leaving the woods, cross to the next footbridge. Go straight ahead. At Padworth Mill, cross the river, the island and more water, to a lane. Turn left, then right before the first house. Follow the lakeside path to the canal. Turn left. At Padworth Lock, cross and return to Aldermaston Wharf.

access information

Aldermaston lies on the A340 Basingstoke to Reading road. Trains between Reading and Newbury stop at Aldermaston about once an hour, Monday to Saturday. For information, phone National Rail Enquiries on 08457 484950 or visit www.railtrack.co.uk.

further information

The Canal Visitors' Centre (0118 971 2868) near the end of the walk has exhibitions and information, plus some refreshments. It is open April to October, Mon–Sat 10 a.m. to 5 p.m. and Sun 2–5 p.m.

As well as wildlife and birds, an encounter with a gently puffing steam barge is likely on a walk alongside the Kennet & Avon canal.

This engraving of the Kennet & Avon Canal gives you a feel for the delightful waterside scenes to be found on this footpath.

Aldermaston Wharf

Froudes Bridge

Wickham Knights Bridge

Kennet and Avon Canal

Padworth Mill

River Kennet

Aldermaston Bridge

A340

Aldermaston

0   1 km   1 mile

▲ Map: Explorer 171
▲ Distance: 7 km/4¼ miles
▲ Walk ID: 81 Liz and David Fishlock

Difficulty rating

Time

▲ Weir, Mill, River, Pub, Toilets, Church, Great Views

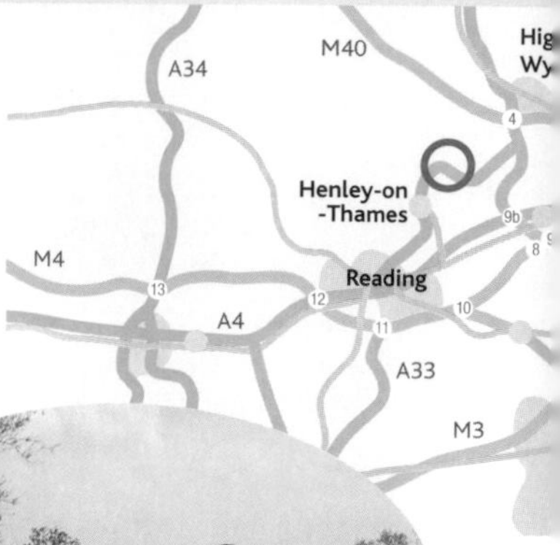

Aston and Remenham from Mill End

This walk crosses the Thames beside Hambleden Weir and Hambleden Mill, follows an open ridge with views across the Thames Valley to the Chiltern Hills, drops down to Remenham and follows the riverside path back to the weir.

1 From the car park, turn right. Just before the junction with the A4155, take the pavement on the right. Cross the road carefully to the footpath that runs between houses on the other side. Follow the footpath signs to pass to the left of Hambleden Mill.

2 Take the footbridge across the weir and then across the lock. Turn left onto the Thames Path. Ignore the right turn shortly after and carry on ahead through the gate to follow the Thames Path, keeping the riverbank on your left.

3 Where the path meets a lane, turn right. At the road junction by the Flower Pot Hotel, turn left and follow the lane to Aston, ignoring a Thames Path sign on your left.

4 Immediately after Highway Cottage, take the path to the right, which crosses a stile then passes to the left of a house to reach a track. Carry on ahead, following the direction of the footpath sign. The clearly defined track crosses open fields to reach a road.

This gentle stroll crosses the weir at Hambleden Mill and provides fine views of the river.

5 Turn right along the road and at the next junction turn left, with Remenham Church on your right. Keeping the church wall on your right, carry on past the lychgate and turn right at the footpath sign, walking along the road until you reach the riverbank.

6 Turn right at the riverbank. Follow the path back to Hambleden Lock, then retrace your steps to the car park.

access information

Mill End lies just east of Henley-on-Thames on the A4155 Henley to Marlow road. Turn left at Mill End towards Hambleden and Skirmett. After about 300 m/328 yards, turn left into the car park.

further information

The picturesque Hambleden Mill has been much photographed, and the walkway that crosses the weir gives beautiful views of the river. From the riverside path on the return route, there are views of Temple Island, which marks the start of the famous Henley Royal Regatta course.

Map labels: M40, High Wy, A34, Henley-on-Thames, M4, Reading, A4, A33, M3

Route map labels: River Thames, Mill End, A4155, Hambleden Mill, Hambleden Lock, Weir, Thames Path, Remenham, Aston

0   1 km   1 mile

▲ Map: Outdoor Leisure 29, 22
▲ Distance: 7.89 km/5 miles
▲ Walk ID: 1327 Graham Hollier

Difficulty rating

Time

▲ Lake, Pub, Toilets, Castle, Wildlife, Birds, Great Views, Butterflies, Mostly Flat, Ancient Monument

Pennington Marshes from Keyhaven

This bracing walk passes through farmland, much of which has been reclaimed from landfill and quarry sites, to pick up the Solent Way for a glorious coastal walk. There is abundant birdlife and wildlife, and wonderful views across to the Isle of Wight.

❶ From the car park, follow a lane almost opposite the Gun Inn, passing Keyhaven Harbour to your right. At a large green gate on your left, cross a broken stile and follow the lane to a council amenity tip. Cross a stile, cross the service road to the tip, and follow the track opposite to a metal gate.

❷ Go past the gate and follow the metalled roadway to another metal gate. Go through a gap to the road. Turn left for a short distance, then cross a stile through the hedge on your right. Follow the footpath, keeping the field edge on your right, to cross another stile towards some houses.

❸ Before you reach the houses, climb a stile in the hedge on your right. Immediately turn left, heading for a path to the left of the fence in front of you. Cross a stile, carry on and cross the next stile. Head for a metalled driveway leading to a road.

❹ Turn left, passing the Chequers pub. Fork right and walk along Platoff Road for a short distance to a bench on your right. Turn right here, signposted 'Maiden Lane', and leading to Normandy Lane. At the next junction, turn right into Maiden Lane.

❺ Follow the road around to the right, through a yacht club yard, passing the clubhouse on the left. Continue on to follow the Solent Way. Carry on along an unmade road, which turns into a path through small trees and shrubs, coming out at a clearing.

❻ Passing a house on your right, turn immediately left over a stile to follow a pathway, keeping the waterway on your left. When you reach a stile, cross it and head for a pair of lock gates. From the gates, follow the sea defence wall back to the start of the walk.

further information

You can extend your walk to include a visit to Hurst Castle, one of the many coastal defences built by Henry VIII. The castle is reached by ferry, which is just a short walk from the car park. Alternatively, you can walk or drive to the start of the shingle spit and walk out to the castle.

access information

Soon after leaving Lymington on the A337 Lymington to New Milton road, branch left towards Lower Pennington and Keyhaven. The walk starts at the car park on the right in Keyhaven, just before the Gun Inn on your left.

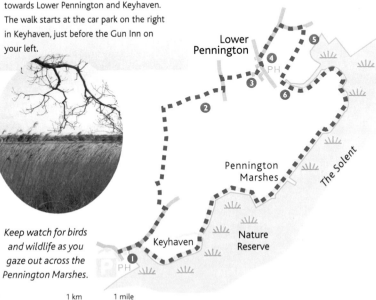

Keep watch for birds and wildlife as you gaze out across the Pennington Marshes.

▲ Map: LRM 175, LRM 186, EXP 145
▲ Distance: 15 km/9¼ miles
▲ Walk ID: 667 Barrie England

Difficulty rating

Time

▲ Lake, Pub, Birds, Great Views

Basingstoke Canal and Surrounding Countryside

Beginning and ending at Winchfield's Barley Mow pub, this walk follows part of the Basingstoke Canal and crosses open countryside. The stretch at Step 6 can be difficult after heavy rain, so an alternative is given in the 'further information'.

1 From the car park, turn left and follow the canal, walking under Blacksmith's Bridge and Double Bridge. Immediately before Chequers Bridge turn left, walk through Crookham Wharf car park, cross the road carefully and turn left, facing the oncoming traffic.

2 Turn left into Stroud Lane. After Willow Cottage, turn left and cross a stream and a stile. Cross the field diagonally left. Cross another stile. Follow the path up across the field, between the pylon and the woods, then down into woodland and across a stream to join a track.

3 Follow the track between the houses. Turn left over a stile and follow the signposted path across the field to two stiles among trees, then onto a track. Continue over another stile. Follow the narrow path between two fences. Cross a left-hand stile into a field and head to the right of a pylon. Follow the path to the road.

4 Cross over and follow the path opposite, beside Double Bridge Farm. Cross a stile and follow the track over Blacksmith's Bridge and down to climb another stile. Turn right, then left to walk beside Tundry Pond. At the bridge, bear left. Cross a stile and after a short distance cross another stile on the right.

5 Fork left and follow the path up across a field towards the barn on the horizon. Follow a track past the barn to the summit, then down past woods and Dogmersfield Lake on the right. Go slightly uphill and across another track to reach two lodges.

6 Turn right immediately after the lodges and follow the path through the woods to the canal. Turn left and follow the path to turn right across the canal bridge. Turn right again and down to follow the canal all the way back to Barley Mow Bridge. Walk under it and turn left to the car park.

access information

Winchfield is on the B3016 south of the M3, off the A30 between Basingstoke and Camberley. The walk starts at the Barley Mow pub. Parking is available at the canal bridge.

A perfect Hampshire day on the Basingstoke Canal – clear blue skies reflecting in the calm waters, brightly coloured barges at rest – make this a memorable and enjoyable walk.

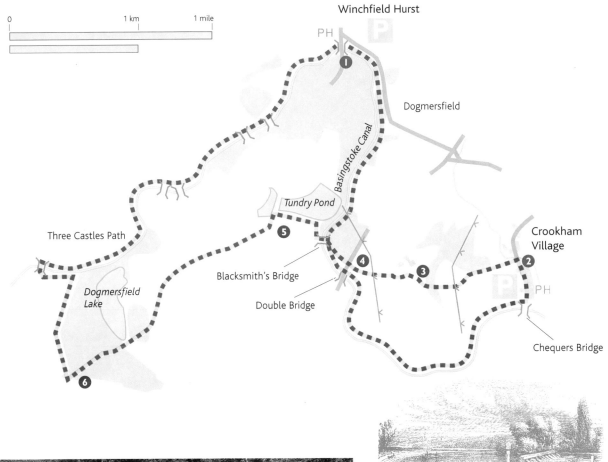

Winchfield Hurst

PH P

① Dogmersfield

Basingstoke Canal

Tundry Pond

Crookham Village

Three Castles Path ⑤

Blacksmith's Bridge

Double Bridge

④ ③ ②

P PH

Dogmersfield Lake

Chequers Bridge

⑥

0 — 1 km — 1 mile

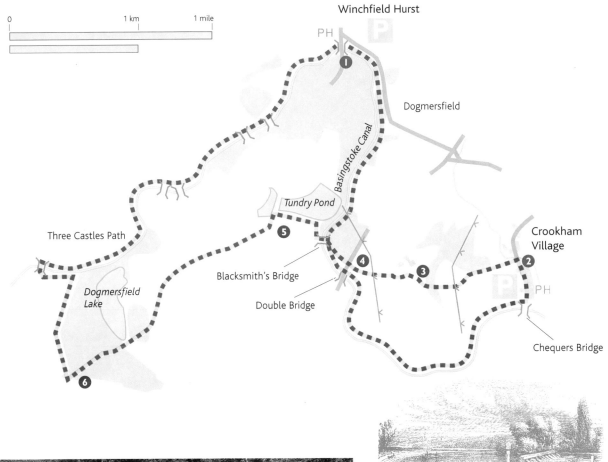

A nostalgic rural scene from the banks of the Basingstoke Canal when barges were used to transport goods along its length.

further information

After heavy rain, at Step 6 continue walking to the main A287. Turn right and stay on the right side of the road to face oncoming traffic. Walk with care, as this is an unpleasant stretch along a fast road. After 750 m/½ mile take the first right at the roundabout and follow this narrow road through Broad Oak to the bridge over the canal.

▲ Map: Explorer 156
▲ Distance: 4.83 km/3 miles
▲ Walk ID: 193 Nigel Vile

Difficulty rating

Time

▲ River, Pub, Toilets, Wildlife, Birds, Flowers

Avoncliff from Bradford-on-Avon via the Kennet & Avon Canal

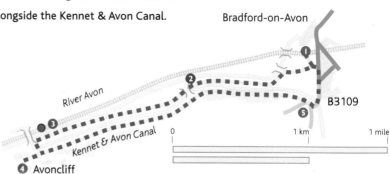

This is a delightful stroll between the Saxon town of Bradford-on-Avon and the hamlet of Avoncliff, deep in the Avon valley. The outward leg follows the banks of the River Avon, the return leg the tow-path alongside the Kennet & Avon Canal.

❶ Walk to the far end of the station car park, to a marker post to 'Tithe Barn and Avoncliff'. Follow the footpath under the railway bridge and across a recreation area to a tarmacked path. Follow the path beside the river to reach a bench and an information board on the right.

❷ Bear right off the path across the grassy area that borders the river (the tarmacked path bears left to the canal). Follow the path beside the river into a meadow. Follow the river downstream across three fields until you reach the weir at Avoncliff.

❸ Where the footpath ends at the weir, climb the steps on the left up to the Kennet & Avon Canal tow-path. At the canal, turn right and follow the tow-path into the hamlet of Avoncliff, and continue until you reach the Avoncliff Aqueduct and the Cross Guns Inn.

❹ Retrace your steps along the tow-path, passing the flight of steps you climbed earlier, and carry on until you reach the Lock Inn Cottage, the Canal Tavern and the B3109 leading into Bradford-on-Avon.

❺ Turn left onto the B3109 and follow the main road back into the town centre. Immediately past the Three Horseshoes Inn, you should turn left to return to the station car park.

access information

The walk starts at the station car park in Bradford-on-Avon. Trains from Bristol and Bath to Portsmouth, Southampton and Weymouth stop here. For motorists, Bradford-on-Avon lies on the A363 between Bath and Trowbridge. The station is clearly signposted from the town centre. A regular bus service from Bath to Trowbridge also passes through Bradford-on-Avon.

further information

The attractive town of Bradford-on-Avon is built in the golden limestone that is typical of this area. The town's heritage includes a tithe barn, a small Saxon church and a lock-up on the Town Bridge, which spans the River Avon.

The weir on the River Avon at Avoncliff. This pretty hamlet has an aqueduct and a friendly inn.

▲ Map: Explorer 121
▲ Distance: 7 km/4¼ miles
▲ Walk ID: 76 Nicholas Rudd-Jones

Difficulty rating

Time

River, Pub, Church, Wildlife,
Great Views

Arundel Castle.

Houghton and River Arun

A3 · A272 · Billingshurst · A29 · A285 · A283 · A27 · Arundel · A27 · Chichester · Brighto

This is a circular walk around the River Arun, taking in the delightful villages of North Stoke and South Stoke on the Sussex Downs above Arundel. If you have time, you can take a detour into Arundel Park.

1 From the small road next to the phone box and post box, take a footpath to the right. Climb two stiles, cross a track and continue on the grassy path downhill. At the bottom of the field, the path becomes gravelled. Cross the footbridge and follow the path as it swings right. Climb the stile and turn left at the river.

2 Climb the next stile to turn right and cross the bridge. Follow the track past the houses and St Leonard's Church in South Stoke. Join the road and swing left past the barn on the right. Turn right off the road and follow the bridleway behind the barn.

3 At the next bridleway signpost, turn left to follow the stony track. Go through a gate and turn right to follow the path around the field edge. Pass the gate back into the woods. Continue past a metal gate leading into Arundel Park on the left. Follow the path along the river, passing under white cliffs.

4 Go through a metal gate at the end of the path and follow the road uphill into Houghton village. At the crossroads, cross the B2139 and follow the minor road signposted to Bury across the fields.

5 Turn right when the South Downs Way crosses the road. At the river, follow the path round to the right to Amberley Bridge. Turn left over the bridge and take the footpath halfway across the bridge

on the right, heading towards North Stoke.

6 Cross a subsidiary bridge, then turn right, back alongside the river. Climb a stile and shortly afterwards take the path to the left. On reaching the North Stoke Road, turn right and return to the start.

further information

The River Arun is tidal and very prone to flooding, so it is a good idea to check the condition before you start out. At Step 4, there is a path alongside the river straight to Houghton Bridge, which can be used to shorten the route in dry weather.

access information

North Stoke lies south of Amberley Station, off the B2139 from Storrington. Parking is available near the phone box in North Stoke. You can also take a train to Amberley (on the Pulborough line from London) and start the walk from there.

South Downs Way · B2139 · Amberley Station · PH · Houghton · **4** · North Stoke · Arundel Park · River Arun · **1** · **2** · **3** · South Stoke · **5** · **6**

0 · 1 km · 1 mile

▲ Map: Explorer 145
▲ Distance: 8.53 km/5¼ miles
▲ Walk ID: 468 Nina Thornhill

Difficulty rating

Time

▲ Pub, Toilets, Wildlife, Birds, Visitor Centre

Brookwood to Aldershot

This walk takes in varied stretches of the Basingstoke Canal. You pass the Deepcut Locks to reach the Great Heath. The canal then runs through the wooded Deepcut Cutting. At the Frimley Aqueduct, the canal widens and barges hug the banks.

❶ At Brookwood station, turn left and cross the road into a side road by the Brookwood Hotel. Cross over the A324 at the end and go down Sheets Heath Lane. At the bridge, cross over and turn left, keeping to the tow-path on the left, not the bridleway. At Pirbright Bridge, go up the slope on the right and then cross the road.

❷ Walk to the first of the Deepcut Locks and cross over it, as the tow-path continues on the opposite bank from this point. Keep ahead on the tow-path at two more bridges. After passing Frimley Lock (no. 28) and cottage, you reach Deepcut Cutting.

❸ Keep ahead along this straight stretch of canal, then walk under a white bridge. After crossing the Frimley Aqueduct, keep ahead at the gate until you reach a fork. You can take either path here, as they both lead to the B3012 ahead.

❹ When you reach the road, turn right and go over the bridge. Cross the road just before the King's Head pub and turn left along the tow-path. Continue to follow the tow-path, with Frimley Lodge Park on your right. If you wish to visit the Basingstoke Canal Visitor Centre further on, cross over to it via a small swing bridge. Otherwise, just keep walking ahead.

❺ Pass under Mytchett Place Bridge, then under Canal Bridge, which comes out by Mytchett Lake. Walk on, passing under two railway bridges. Just after the second of these, you come to a gap on your right. Turn right through the gap into Ash Vale station car park.

access information

The walk runs from Brookwood to Ash Vale railway stations, and can be followed in either direction. Both stations are on the Waterloo to Alton line and car parking is available at both, although Brookwood is larger.

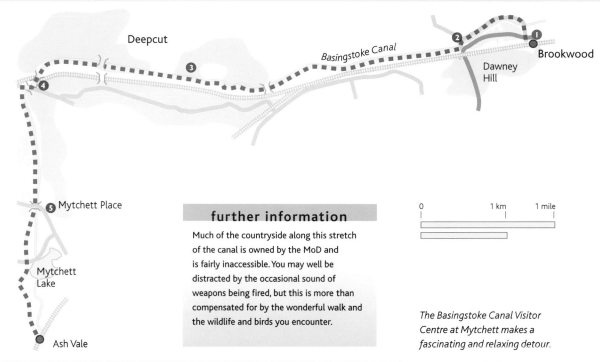

Deepcut

Basingstoke Canal

Brookwood

Dawney
Hill

Mytchett Place

Mytchett
Lake

Ash Vale

further information

Much of the countryside along this stretch
of the canal is owned by the MoD and
is fairly inaccessible. You may well be
distracted by the occasional sound of
weapons being fired, but this is more than
compensated for by the wonderful walk and
the wildlife and birds you encounter.

0   1 km   1 mile

*The Basingstoke Canal Visitor
Centre at Mytchett makes a
fascinating and relaxing detour.*

▲ Map: Explorer 160
▲ Distance: 8.86 km/5½ miles
▲ Walk ID: 736 Tony Brotherton

Difficulty rating

Time

▲ Lake, Pub, Toilets, Wildlife, Birds, Flowers, Great Views

Around Virginia Water

This walk around Virginia Water, in Windsor Great Park, has some stunning vistas. The Valley Gardens are one of the world's best woodland gardens. Detours from the main route given here will reveal many interesting features and landmarks.

❶ From Blacknest car park, walk ahead on the broad woodland path to reach the lake opposite the stone bridge. Turn right to follow the lakeside path, eventually passing the 'ruins' to your right. Walk on to the cascade, and continue downhill.

❷ Cross the stone bridge and look out for the 'hidden' path between the rhododendrons on the left. Climb a short path to rejoin the lakeside path and walk past the Wheatsheaf car park. Carry on alongside the lake to the totem-pole. From here, take the sand and gravel path uphill towards Valley Gardens.

❸ Near the top of the gardens, turn right to reach a signpost at a cross-paths. Follow the 'Savill Gardens' sign through parkland to a five-fingered signpost. Take the path to Obelisk Pond. Follow the path around the pond, then continue to cross a balustraded bridge.

❹ When the path gives way to grass, bear half-left between trees to follow the edge of a wood on your left. Heading towards the equestrian statue, reach the crossroads at the corner of Smith's Lawn. Turn left, and follow the rail fence, with the grandstand ahead.

❺ Go left at the 'Guards Polo Club' sign. Bear right to re-enter Valley Gardens and continue to the heather garden entrance. Go into the heather garden and bear left along the broad grass path. Leave the garden through either of two gates, taking the path to the right back to the five-fingered signpost. Follow the sandy path half-right into woods, then a broad grassy swathe back to the lake path.

❻ Follow the lake path, finally turning left to join the road between the main lake and Johnson's Pond. Leave the road to walk alongside the horse gallop, then rejoin the road to cross the stone bridge. Bear left on the path back to the lakeside. Go ahead on the woodland path to Blacknest car park, or turn left for the Wheatsheaf car park.

further information

There are no stiles, brambles or nettles on this walk – just a few gentle slopes, rhododendrons, azaleas and magnolias in spring, and a fantastic variety of birdlife both on and around the lake. Look out for green woodpeckers, kingfishers, herons and great-crested grebes, as well as exotic ducks and geese.

Enjoy the abundant floral delights in the peaceful surroundings of Virginia Water.

access information

The route passes close to the three main
car parks that serve the park. They are
at Blacknest (current charge £1.50),
Wheatsheaf (current charge £3.50) and
Savill Gardens (current charge £2.00).
There is free verge car parking at Mill Lane.
Wheatsheaf car park is accessible by buses
between Bagshot and Egham.

Visit the nearby
Windsor Castle,
the splendid royal
residence of Queen
Elizabeth II.

▲ Map: Explorer 145 Guildford and Farnham

▲ Distance: 8.05 km/5 miles

▲ Walk ID: 31 Daisy Hayden

Difficulty rating

Time

▲ Canal, Toilets, National Trust/NTS, Birds

Guildford to Godalming

This is a beautiful, relaxing and easy walk along the River Wey, including the Godalming navigations. The open valley is National Trust land, and the scenery is both varied and unspoilt.

access information

The walk starts at Guildford railway station (instructions are given from the down-line – if you are travelling towards London, cross over the line to start). Trains run from Waterloo to Guildford every 40 minutes and return from Godalming to Waterloo every 50 minutes. There are two or three trains every hour.

The ideal antidote to the stresses and strains of everyday life – the calm, gentle backwaters of the River Wey.

These beautifully restored narrowboats are a frequent and charming sight on this stretch of the River Wey.

❶ Turn right out of the station, walk down Park Street and cross Farnham Road, heading for the church in the distance. Turn left into the High Street and pass the church to reach the White Horse pub. Go through the pub beer garden and take the riverbank path to the right, to a white bridge. Cross this towards Millmead Lock.

❷ Do not cross the lock, but stay on the path, following the sign to Godalming on the right. Cross a bridge, passing some boathouses. The river loops to the left, then curves right. Follow the path on the right to join the river by a bridge, or follow the bend of the river to the same bridge.

❸ Turn right across the bridge to follow the riverbank path. Carry on, crossing another bridge. If you are not detouring across the bridge to visit the nature reserve at St Catherine's Lock, continue on the riverside path. Where the railway crosses the river, walk under the bridge.

❹ Cross over the A248 at Broadford Bridge and keep following the path ahead. At the next bridge, after Unstead Lock, cross the road over the bridge to follow the footpath sign. Continue past an old brick footbridge, and carry on straight over the next bridge towards Godalming.

❺ Follow the path to the car park, then turn left over the bridge. Just after the bridge, go straight ahead. Turn right at the top of the road for the main high street and follow signs to the station. Alternatively, just after the bridge turn right along Bury Road and take the path to the right off the road, on the left of St Peter and St Paul Church, to the station.

further information

It is wise to wear boots or wellies on this walk, as the path gets muddy. If you are walking with children, it is fun for them to watch or help the boat people operate the lock gates at Unstead Lock. At St Catherine's Lock, cross the bridge if you wish to visit the nature reserve. Take care crossing the roads at Step 4, as the traffic is very fast here.

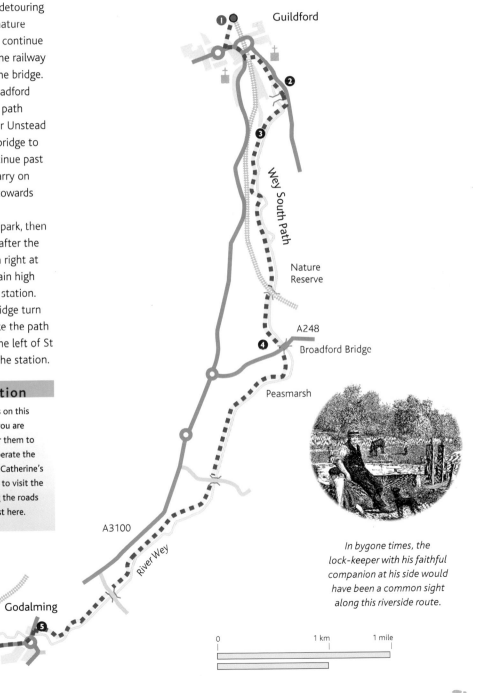

Guildford

Wey South Path

Nature Reserve

A248

Broadford Bridge

Peasmarsh

A3100

River Wey

Godalming

In bygone times, the lock-keeper with his faithful companion at his side would have been a common sight along this riverside route.

0   1 km   1 mile

▲ Map: Explorer 161
▲ Distance: 14 km/8¾ miles
▲ Walk ID: 511 Oliver O'Brien

Difficulty rating

🐾🐾🐾

Time

●●●●

▲ River, Pub, Toilets, Museum, Play Area, Stately Home, Botanic Gardens, Wildlife, Birds, Flowers, Great Views

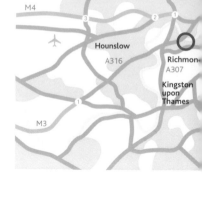

Richmond and Kew

This circular walk takes in a meander of the Thames, so that most of it is beside the river. Starting at Mortlake, the route joins the Thames Path. The return leg takes in the north end of Richmond Park, with a short stretch through a residential area.

❶ From the station, walk into Mortlake Green and take the path to the left across the park. Cross the road and follow the Budweiser Brewery access road ahead, signposted 'Thames Cycle Route'. Pass The Ship pub and turn left towards Kew Bridge to follow the path beside the river.

❷ Staying on the path when it bears away from the road, pass under Chiswick Bridge and continue past the Public Record Office. Pass under Kew Rail Bridge and carry on past Kew Gardens Pier and under Kew Road Bridge.

❸ Just after Kew Bridge, pass the sign indicating the Kew Gardens entrance, and another pier. Continue along the tow-path beside the river, passing another entrance to the gardens. Crossing the Meridian Line, the route continues along the path, with water on both sides.

❹ Pass Richmond Lock, cross the Meridian Line again, and continue along the path, passing under Twickenham Bridge, a railway bridge and Richmond Bridge. When the path leaves the river, follow it through a small park and pass a small flight of steps on the left.

❺ Go straight ahead, through a set of gates and across a field. After a house, turn left and cross the main road. Follow the path opposite steeply uphill. At the top, turn right on another road.

access information

This walk starts at Mortlake railway station, which is served by South Western trains and is accessible from central London. If you are travelling by car, there is very limited parking at the station. An alternative is to park in Richmond town centre and head west across Richmond Green to the river.

An enchanting glimpse of the River Thames across the lush countryside from Richmond Hill.

The walk passes the Public Records Office, Kew Bridge, the Royal Botanic Gardens at Kew and the Royal Observatory at Richmond, which is built on the Meridian Line. Kew Gardens are the world's largest and most famous botanic gardens and are well worth a visit (there is an entrance fee).

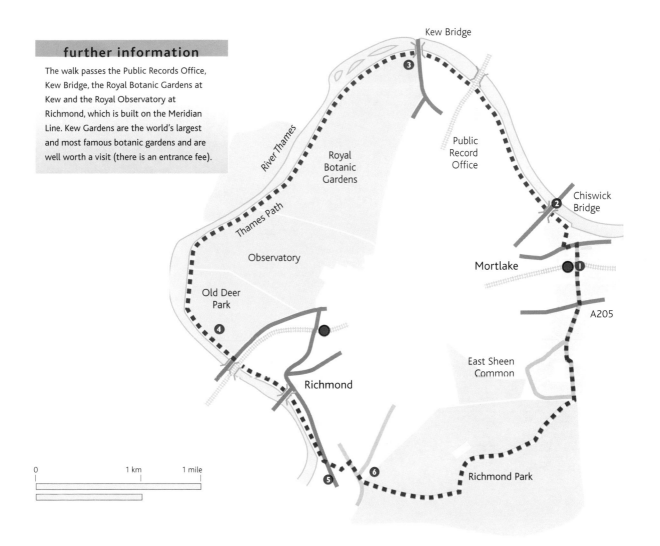

Kew Bridge

River Thames

Royal Botanic Gardens

Thames Path

Public Record Office

Chiswick Bridge

Observatory

Mortlake

Old Deer Park

A205

Richmond

East Sheen Common

0   1 km   1 mile

Richmond

Richmond Park

6 Carry on ahead at the first mini-roundabout, then turn left at the next into Richmond Park. Go straight on at the next mini-roundabout and follow the path to the left of the road. Turn left towards Holly Lodge (Bog Lodge), then bear right just before the lodge and follow the path to Sheen Gate. Walk up Sheen Lane (B351), cross Upper Richmond Road West (A205) at the traffic lights, and continue along Sheen Lane back to Mortlake station.

When passing through the picturesque Richmond Park, herds of deer are a common sight.

▲ Map: Explorer 161
▲ Distance: 9.5 km/6 miles
▲ Walk ID: 1188 Oliver O'Brien

Difficulty rating

Time

▲ River, Lake, Pub, Toilets, Stately Home, Wildlife, Birds, Flowers, Butterflies, Food Shop

Hampton Court Park and Bushy Park

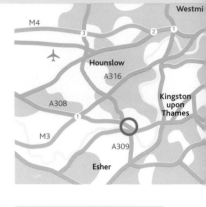

This walk winds through Bushy Park, follows the Thames Path upstream from Hampton Wick, and goes through Hampton Court Palace Gardens, past the palace's east front, before returning to the start over Hampton Court Green.

❶ From the car park, turn right, then turn right again through heavy black gates into Bushy Park. Follow the faint path through the rough parkland. Where the path meets a metalled road, continue straight ahead through fenced woodlands and cross a small bridge over a stream. Continue along the road.

❷ Where five paths meet, turn sharp right and follow a small path to a gate. Pass through it and follow the path through woodland, passing several small ponds. Just before the path crosses a bridge, bear right and go through the gate. Turn left and walk through open parkland to the road.

❸ Turn right to the Diana Fountain. When you reach the fountain, head back up to the left towards a lake. Bear slightly right of the car park access road and cross towards the lake. Follow the path, keeping the lake on your left. Cross a bridge over a stream and immediately bear right, following the path around a small wood.

❹ Where the path meets a metalled road, turn right and follow it past a lake and over a bridge. At the road, go through the gate and bear right, following the road around to the right. At the roundabout, cross over and walk up to the bridge.

❺ Turn right off the road onto the Thames Path. Follow the road to meet the track, with the river on your left. Continue to follow the path along the river to Hampton Court Palace Gardens. Turn right through the gate and follow the track parallel to the road.

❻ Bear right at the next junction, then bear left through the gardens to the east front. Follow the wide avenue past the palace. Turn left through a gate signposted 'Maze' and continue ahead, passing through three gates. When you reach the road, cross to Hampton Court Green and follow the path back to the car park where you started.

access information

The walk starts at Hampton Court Green car park, the main car park for visitors to Hampton Court Palace, on the A308. If travelling by train, go to Hampton Wick station and start the walk at Step 5. Some London buses serving Hounslow pass near Hampton Court Palace.

Hampton Court Palace, one of the most historic buildings that borders the River Thames.

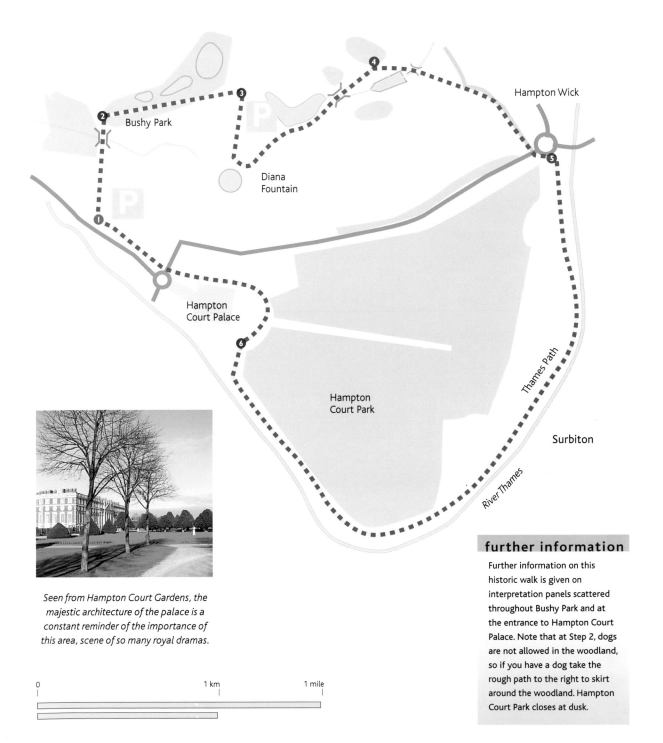

Bushy Park

Hampton Wick

Diana
Fountain

Hampton
Court Palace

Hampton
Court Park

Thames Path

Surbiton

River Thames

*Seen from Hampton Court Gardens, the
majestic architecture of the palace is a
constant reminder of the importance of
this area, scene of so many royal dramas.*

0   1 km   1 mile

further information

Further information on this
historic walk is given on
interpretation panels scattered
throughout Bushy Park and at
the entrance to Hampton Court
Palace. Note that at Step 2, dogs
are not allowed in the woodland,
so if you have a dog take the
rough path to the right to skirt
around the woodland. Hampton
Court Park closes at dusk.

▲ Map: Explorer 192

▲ Distance: 8.05 km/5 miles

▲ Walk ID: 1183 Brian and Anne Sandland

Difficulty rating

Time

▲ Pub, Toilets, Church, Wildlife, Birds, Flowers, Butterflies, Great Views, Industrial Archaeology

The Grand Union Canal and Great Brickhill from Three Locks Inn

From the Three Locks Inn, this walk follows the tow-path of the Grand Union Canal, then crosses fields to Great Brickhill village on a ridge with great views. From here, the route follows a bridleway to rejoin the tow-path and return to the start point.

❶ From the car park, cross the road and go down to the canal tow-path. Follow the path to the first bridge, then cross the canal and continue on the opposite bank. Pass the lock at Stoke Hammond and carry on under the bridge. Continue for some distance to the next bridge. Look for an exit to the right and climb the steps to the road.

❷ Turn right and follow the road. Cross the river bridges, then Lower Rectory Farm on your right. Opposite the entrance to Westfield Farm on your left, turn right onto a signposted path. Go through the metal gate and follow the broad path diagonally left across the field, then bear right to follow trees and a hedge on your left. Cross a fence and bear left.

❸ Follow an old wall on your left, cross a stile by a metal gate, then head for the further of two Scots pines to reach another gate just after a yellow way-mark. Beyond the gate, follow a track between hedges. Go through another gate and turn left onto the tarmacked lane, past Great Brickhill Church. At the T-junction, turn right into Lower Way.

The Grand Union Canal is a modern man-made wonder and is enjoyed today for a variety of leisure activities.

access information

The Three Locks car park and picnic site is on the east side of the A4146 between Bletchley and Leighton Buzzard.

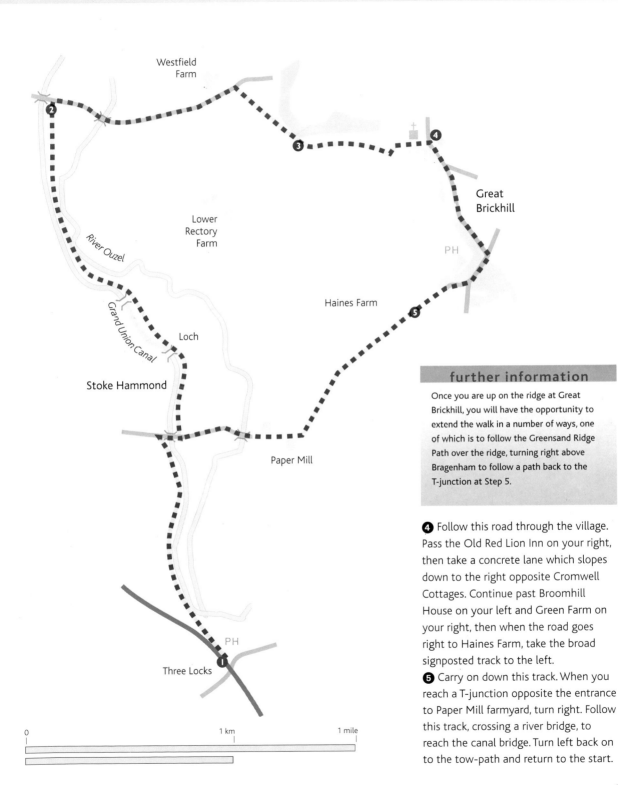

Westfield
Farm

Lower
Rectory
Farm

River Ouzel

Grand Union Canal

Loch

Stoke Hammond

Paper Mill

Great
Brickhill

PH

Haines Farm

Three Locks

PH

0   1 km   1 mile

further information

Once you are up on the ridge at Great
Brickhill, you will have the opportunity to
extend the walk in a number of ways, one
of which is to follow the Greensand Ridge
Path over the ridge, turning right above
Bragenham to follow a path back to the
T-junction at Step 5.

❹ Follow this road through the village.
Pass the Old Red Lion Inn on your right,
then take a concrete lane which slopes
down to the right opposite Cromwell
Cottages. Continue past Broomhill
House on your left and Green Farm on
your right, then when the road goes
right to Haines Farm, take the broad
signposted track to the left.

❺ Carry on down this track. When you
reach a T-junction opposite the entrance
to Paper Mill farmyard, turn right. Follow
this track, crossing a river bridge, to
reach the canal bridge. Turn left back on
to the tow-path and return to the start.

▲ Map: Explorer 172
▲ Distance: 10.47 km/6½ miles
▲ Walk ID: 24 Daisy Hayden

Difficulty rating

Time

▲ River, Pub, Stately Home, Wildlife,
Great Views

Chess Valley from Chalfont and Latimer

This is a peaceful and beautiful river-valley walk in an area of outstanding natural beauty on the edge of the Chilterns. The route goes through Latimer village, with its picture-postcard village green, then passes Chenies Manor, returning to Chalfont.

❶ From the station, take the first right turn. Follow this road straight ahead, crossing another road, to reach the wood. Go through a gap in the fence and take the path, straight on but slightly to the right, downhill through the wood.

❷ Go straight across the field, cross the road and bear right across another field. Cross the river and turn immediately right. Climb the stile and follow the river to a gate to Latimer and a stile. Cross the stile and go left over another stile, following the Chess Valley Walk.

❸ After Mill Farmyard, turn left along the road, then right across a stile. Follow the Chess Valley Walk to a junction. Go straight ahead, turn right by a white house, then follow the road left. Climb a stile on the right and walk across the right side of the field. Cross the next field diagonally left. Follow the path uphill through the trees.

❹ Go straight ahead, following a holly hedge, cross a stile, and go through a gate into the churchyard. Turn right and follow a footpath sign to Chorleywood. Cross a road and a stile. Head straight downhill, then turn right to the end of the field. Turn left to cross the river, then a stream.

❺ Carry on to a signpost and head towards Chenies. Cross two stiles, then walk diagonally up across the field on your right to the far corner. Go through the gap in the hedge. Follow the left-hand field edge, then follow the farm track to the main road. Cross over, then cross the village green.

❻ Follow the lane to the church, then turn right. Follow the walled path to a stile. Follow the path left through the wood, then go straight ahead to join a wide track through fields and woods to a road. Turn right, then cross to follow a footpath on the left through the wood. At the gap in Step 1, return to the start.

access information

The walk starts at Chalfont and Latimer tube station, which is an hour from London on the Metropolitan line from Central London – take the Amersham train. From this direction, cross the tracks using the subway and go down the steep steps to Bedford Avenue, then turn left for 200 m/182 yards to the start of the walk. Car parking is available at the tube station.

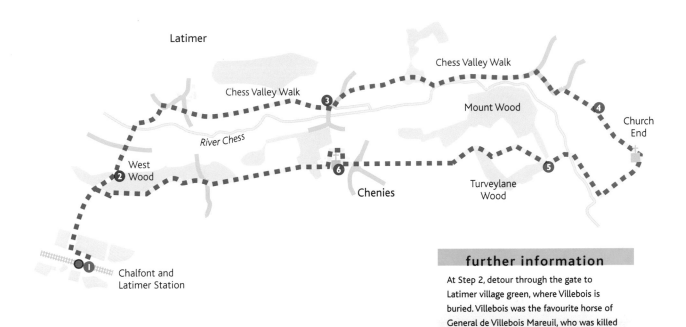

Latimer

Chess Valley Walk

Chess Valley Walk

3

Mount Wood

River Chess

4

Church End

West Wood

2

6

Chenies

Turveylane Wood

5

Chalfont and Latimer Station

1

0   1 km   1 mile

The serenity of the River Chess flowing calmly on its way near the Buckinghamshire village of Latimer.

further information

At Step 2, detour through the gate to Latimer village green, where Villebois is buried. Villebois was the favourite horse of General de Villebois Mareuil, who was killed defending the life of Charles Compton Cavendish, Lord Chesham of Latimer, in the Boer War. Lord Chesham brought the horse back to England, where it died in 1811.

▲ Map: Explorer 184
▲ Distance: 8.05 km/5 miles
▲ Walk ID: 1125 Brian and Anne Sandland

Difficulty rating

Time

River, Sea, Toilets, Play Area, Church, Wildlife, Birds, Flowers, Great Views, Butterflies, Café, Gift Shop, Food Shop, Public Transport, Restaurant

The Naze and Cormorant Creek from Walton Station

This circular walk starts beside the sea, going through the little resort of Walton, then across the open space of the Naze. You then turn alongside Cormorant Creek to reach the backwater of Walton Channel and return beside Walton Hall Marshes.

1 From the station, follow the road to the seafront, then continue ahead with the sea on your right.

2 Continue along the coast, and turn right into East Terrace to stay close to the sea. When the road ends, just after the coastguard station and the old lifeboat house, take the tarmacked path, then Cliff Parade. When this road ends, continue on the grass, rising slightly but still staying close to the sea. Just after a shelter on your right, bear right.

3 Head initially towards the sea, but bear left along a path to the seaward side of bungalows to follow a footpath above the sea. Bear left again when you reach steps down, then after a short distance go right on a broad gravel track to head towards a tall brick tower.

4 Continue, still close to the cliff-edge, along a wide area of mown grass. The mown path bears left and right around a cliff fall, then continues ahead in the direction of Felixstowe.

5 Carry on between bushes on a very narrow path close to the cliff-edge, but when this ends turn inland for a short distance to another, wider path and turn right, still heading towards Felixstowe. When you reach a raised bank, climb this and turn left onto tarmac.

6 At the end of the tarmac bear left, still on the raised bank. Follow the path alongside Cormorant Creek, then along the backwater of Walton Channel, with Walton Hall Marshes on your left. The riverbank eventually brings you to a bend on a road via a field-edge path. Turn right and follow the road back towards the town centre. Retrace your steps along the seafront and back to the station.

access information

The walk starts at Walton-on-the-Naze train station – trains run from London Liverpool Street station. By car, follow the A120 east from Colchester, then signs to Walton-on-the-Naze. Buses run to Walton from Colchester or Clacton.

A dramatic view of the Naze Nature Reserve, an area rich in its diversity of indigenous and migratory birds.

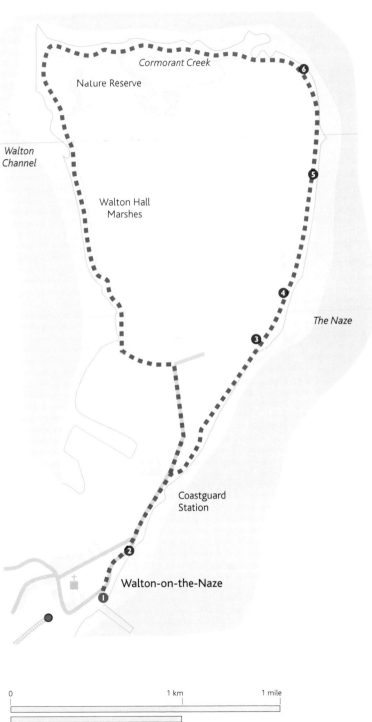

Cormorant Creek

Nature Reserve

6

Walton
Channel

5

Walton Hall
Marshes

4

The Naze

3

Coastguard
Station

2

Walton-on-the-Naze

1

further information

Walton is a small, old-fashioned seaside resort just north of Clacton and Frinton. The Naze on which it stands is an area of open land fronting the North Sea. There is much wildlife here, and a great variety of birdlife. The cliffs on the seaward edge of the Naze are a favourite haunt of geologists and fossil hunters.

0		1 km	1 mile

▲ Map: Explorer 184
▲ Distance: 9.66 km/6 miles
▲ Walk ID: 1028 Brian and Anne Sandland

Difficulty rating

Time

▲ River, Lake, Pub, Church, Wildlife, Birds, Flowers, Great Views, Butterflies, Food Shop, Industrial Archaeology, Mostly Flat, Tea Shop, Woodland

River Colne and Alresford Creek from Wivenhoe

This walk starts at Wivenhoe and follows the River Colne seawards, mainly along a former railway track enticingly known as the 'Crab and Winkle Line'. The route then turns away from the river and returns to Wivenhoe through fields and woodland.

Wivenhoe and the River Colne, popular with boat lovers of all tastes.

❶ From the station, walk along West Street, then turn right into Bath Street. Turn left at the quay and walk on, keeping the river to your right. Take the concrete path to the left of the rusting shipbuilding shed, then bear right along a tarmac road, passing the Colne Barrier.

❷ Follow the gravel path past Wivenhoe Sailing Club. Go through a gate and follow the raised path by the river. Cross a stile, walk through the trees, then continue parallel to the river. Where the path forks, bear left, with Alresford Creek to your right, to meet a road.

❸ Turn left and walk past the sand and gravel workings. At the brow of the hill, turn left along a signposted bridleway. At the next junction, continue on the track to the right beside the concrete road. After passing Marsh Farm, turn right and continue along the road.

❹ Follow a signposted path left over a stile. Cross the railway, then turn left to reach a sandy track. After a short distance, take a right-hand path through the trees, crossing a stream to follow it on your left. Cross a bridge, then climb and descend steps. Follow the stream to a stile and a lane.

access information

The walk starts at Wivenhoe railway station. Wivenhoe is on the London Liverpool Street to Clacton line and there is an hourly service in both directions. Wivenhoe lies south of the A133 from Colchester to Clacton. Turn right onto the B1027, then fork right onto the B1028.

further information

Wivenhoe was formerly a shipbuilding town and the walk passes the site of the old shipyard. There is also an impressive barrage, built to prevent tidal surges reaching Wivenhoe and Colchester, further upriver. The water-filled pits of disused sand and gravel workings provide homes for a variety of wildfowl and wildlife.

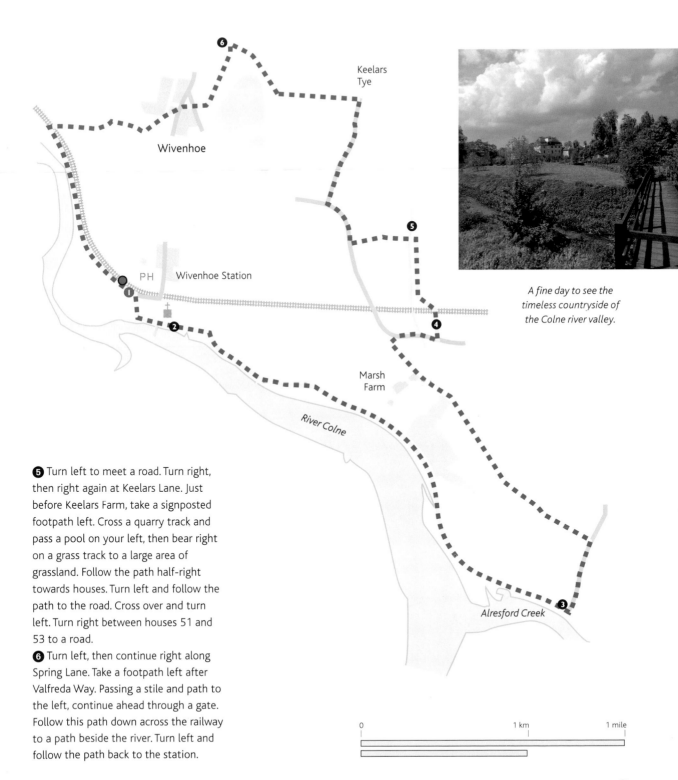

Keelars
Tye

Wivenhoe

PH   Wivenhoe Station

Marsh
Farm

River Colne

Alresford Creek

A fine day to see the timeless countryside of the Colne river valley.

❺ Turn left to meet a road. Turn right, then right again at Keelars Lane. Just before Keelars Farm, take a signposted footpath left. Cross a quarry track and pass a pool on your left, then bear right on a grass track to a large area of grassland. Follow the path half-right towards houses. Turn left and follow the path to the road. Cross over and turn left. Turn right between houses 51 and 53 to a road.

❻ Turn left, then continue right along Spring Lane. Take a footpath left after Valfreda Way. Passing a stile and path to the left, continue ahead through a gate. Follow this path down across the railway to a path beside the river. Turn left and follow the path back to the station.

0		1 km		1 mile

▲ Map: Explorer 138
▲ Distance: 7 km/4¼ miles
▲ Walk ID: 1048 Ian Elmes

Difficulty rating

Time

▲ Wildlife, Birds, Flowers, Great Views, Butterflies

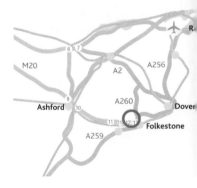

Castle Hill

Ancient meets modern on this short circular walk above Folkestone, which begins at a viewpoint, then takes a pleasant route along part of the North Downs Way, taking in views of the English Channel and overlooking the Channel Tunnel Terminal.

The English Channel with the impressive Channel Tunnel in the foreground.

1 From the viewpoint, go through the kissing gate and turn left. Follow signs for the North Downs Way and Saxon Shore Way. Continue along the footpath, alongside the road, then follow the signs through a gate heading towards Castle Lane. Passing a stile on the left, continue along the footpath.

2 Go through a kissing gate and follow the path to the top of Castle Lane. Turn right for a short distance down Castle Hill, then take a footpath to the left. Follow the path round to the left, through kissing gates and up the hill past the pylon.

3 At the next waymarker, keep left on the North Downs Way. Follow the path, and at the next waymarker, keep straight ahead. At the bottom of the path, where the road meets the footpath, go through the right-hand gate and keep to the path bearing right.

4 Walk up and over the hill and down the other side. Keep to the fence on your left. At the bottom, turn right, following the footpath down and then up some steps. Follow the path, keeping right at the waymarkers, signposted Countryside Project. Carry on downhill for some distance, then turn right at the next waymarker.

5 Follow the path up the steps and diagonally left to the next waymarker, following more steep winding steps. At the next waymarker, turn left, following the blue arrow. This path crosses the A20. Follow the path round to the kissing gate.

6 Turn left at the kissing gate, following the path towards Castle Hill and Caesar's Camp, then follow the lower path on the left to the bottom of Castle Hill. At the end of the path, go through the gate and turn right up the road, then right again up Castle Hill. At the top, turn left and return to the viewpoint.

access information

Leave the M20 at Junction 13 and follow the signs for Folkestone (A259). At the third roundabout left onto Canterbury Road, continue up the hill and turn left on the Pilgrims Way. Follow the road along and into Crete Road West. The viewpoint is on the left by a lay-by.

▲ Map: Explorer 184

▲ Distance: 6.44 km/4 miles

▲ Walk ID: 1213 Brian and Anne Sandland

Difficulty rating

Time

▲ Toilets, Play Area, Church, Wildlife, Birds, Flowers, Butterflies, Mostly Flat, Public Transport, Restaurant, Tea Shop, Ancient Monument

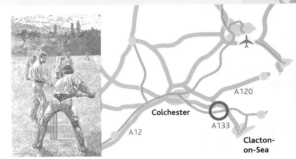

Frating Abbey and Aingers Green from Great Bentley

Great Bentley is a charming village with the largest village green in the country, where cricket is played in summer. This walk follows field paths to Frating Abbey, then lanes and more field and woodland tracks and paths all the way back.

❶ From the station, walk towards the village, then fork left at the village green towards the church. Walk through the churchyard, keeping the church on your left. Go through a gate in the hedge and turn left. Go through two more gates then turn right with a wire fence on your right.

❷ Follow a fence then a ditch bearing left. Cross the ditch over a concrete bridge and turn left. Bear right for a short distance by the embankment, then cross a stile on the left to continue along a narrow path. At the foot crossing, go over the railway, then a stile.

❸ Walk between fields with a ditch on your right. Cross the ditch and continue with the ditch on your left. When the ditch ends, turn right towards farm buildings. Follow the farm track to the road and turn left, past Frating Abbey. Continue to a signposted path left.

❹ Cross the field to the far side, then follow the arrow to cross two bridges, then a stile. Cross a narrow field and another stile. After a short distance, turn left on a path curving right to a grass path. Follow the grass path up the rise.

❺ At the woodland, turn right, then left over a track to a track between the trees. Follow this to a road at Aingers Green. Cross to follow Weeley Road to a

junction, and take a left turn signposted Tendring. Follow the lane to St Mary's Farm and turn left, passing the farm on a signposted footpath.

❻ Follow the path towards the railway. Just before the railway, turn left, then right over a footbridge. Cross a narrow section of field, then the railway. Follow a tarmacked path to a road and bear right on Pine Close. At a junction, bear right again to a footpath between fences. At the road, turn left and walk beside the village green to the Plough Inn. Turn left to the station.

Great Bentley village green and the very essence of English life – a game of cricket.

access information

Great Bentley lies south of the A133 Colchester to Clacton Road. The walk starts at the railway station, which is served by trains from London Liverpool Street. Car parking is available outside the station. Great Bentley is also accessible by buses running between Colchester and Clacton.

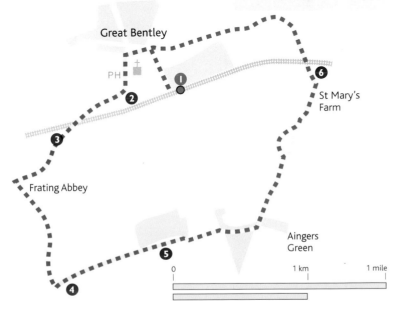

▲ Map: Explorer 196
▲ Distance: 12.88 km/8 miles
▲ Walk ID: 1352 Brian and Anne Sandland

Difficulty rating

Time

▲ Lake, Church, Wildlife, Birds, Flowers, Great Views, Butterflies, Mostly Flat, Woodland

Tye Green and Rivers Hall from Boxted

The beginning and end of this walk follow sections of the Essex Way through delightful countryside in an area of outstanding natural beauty, giving superb views at various points. You pass at least six farms and a number of magnificent halls.

A summer scene stretching below Langham Church near Boxted.

❶ From the car park, walk back towards the road, then turn right to take the signposted path. At the field end, bear right, passing wooden barns, then fork left by a pond. Follow a track past Boxted Hall, then turn left at a road. Take the right turn at the T-junction with Church Road and continue.

❷ Turn left on a footpath opposite Kerseys. At the field end, cross a footbridge. Follow the track ahead to Green Lane. Turn right, then left on a footpath. Follow the right field edge to a signpost in a hollow. Turn right across the field to pass through Holly Lodge Farm to the road. Turn left and walk through Tye Green.

❸ Turn left on a footpath opposite Preen View. Just before farm buildings, bear diagonally left across a field. Cross a track. Go through a hedge, then a field, a hedge and a field to pass Barritts Farm on the right. Follow the drive to a road. Turn left.

❹ Turn right at the next signposted path, which bears right to another road. Turn left. Turn right on the footpath opposite a pond. Follow the field edge to a telegraph pole, then bear right to pass Plains Farm on your left. Continue ahead across the field. Turn left into Cage Lane, turning left at the sharp bend.

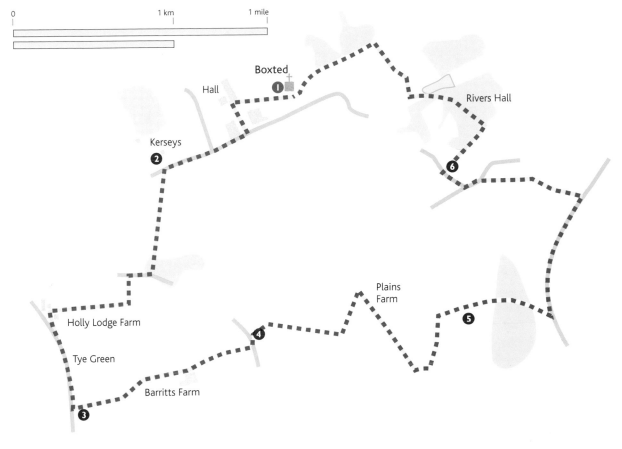

Boxted

Hall

Kerseys ❷

Rivers Hall

❻

Holly Lodge Farm

Tye Green

Barritts Farm

❸

Plains Farm

❺

❹

❺ Turn right and follow a track signed 'Unsuitable for Motor Vehicles' through trees and across to a road. Turn left and follow the road down through woodland then up. At the top of the hill, follow a footpath left across two fields to Dedham Road. Turn left, then right into Cooks Hill.

❻ Turn right and follow the footpath to meet a track. Turn left towards Rivers Hall. Follow the footpath left then right around the outbuildings. When you meet the drive by the moat, turn left downhill through woodland, past a lake, then up. Turn left along Church Street to Boxted. At the bend by Aubrey Cottages, follow the path ahead back to the start.

further information

At Step 2 you pass an interesting vineyard with opportunities for wine-tasting and/or purchase. The walk can be shortened by turning left at the end of Step 3, then following a signposted footpath left at Boxted British Legion Hut, past a lake and back to the start point.

access information

Boxted lies east of the A134 Colchester to Sudbury road, and can be reached via a number of signposted turnings. Follow signs to the village and park in the car park by the church and school.

Take time to visit the 12th-century Church of St Peter's in Boxted, with its splendid square Norman tower and dormer windows.

▲ Map: Outdoor Leisure 29

▲ Distance: 8 km/5 miles

▲ Walk ID: 546 David L. White

Difficulty rating

Time

▲ Hills, Sea, Pub, Toilets, Church, Wildlife, Birds, Flowers, Great Views

Niton and St Catherine's Down from Blackgang

This walk is in an area with a seafaring history, with three lighthouses from different periods and a smuggling tradition around Blackgang and Niton. Blackgang now clings precariously to the cliff-edge, slowly disappearing as the cliff erodes.

① From the seaward side of the car park, climb up some steps and follow the path to the cliff top. Turn left towards Niton and follow the path past the radio mast station. After the second stile beyond the radio station, turn immediately left over another stile, heading inland.

The southern coastline of the Isle of Wight with Blackgang and most of the walk area visible.

② Keeping the fence on your right, walk across the field to a stile at the far side. Cross a small meadow, bearing slightly left, to climb another stile. Walk through a coppice path to the main road. Follow the road to the right until it bears left, marked 'Through traffic', to the church. At the lychgate, turn left and go up Pan Lane. When the lane becomes a bridle path, carry on, turning left at a junction of paths.

access information

Blackgang lies just off the southern tip of the Isle of Wight, off the A3055. There is a large car park. The nearest bus stop is Blackgang. If you are travelling by ferry from the mainland, the best crossings are the Portsmouth/Ryde catamaran, the Southsea/Ryde hovercraft and the Portsmouth/Fishbourne car ferry.

3 Go through a metal gate and follow a blue arrow straight ahead. Go through another metal gate at the far side of the field. (At this point you can turn right and walk across the field, bearing slightly right towards a signpost, then follow a bridleway to Hoy's Monument. Return to the gate to continue the walk at Step 4.)

4 Turn immediately left and climb to the summit of the hill, where the Old Oratory stands, for fantastic views. The Old Oratory was one of the original lighthouses, built in 1314. From the Old Oratory, cross the field, heading towards the sea, to climb a stile. Follow the path down to the start of the walk.

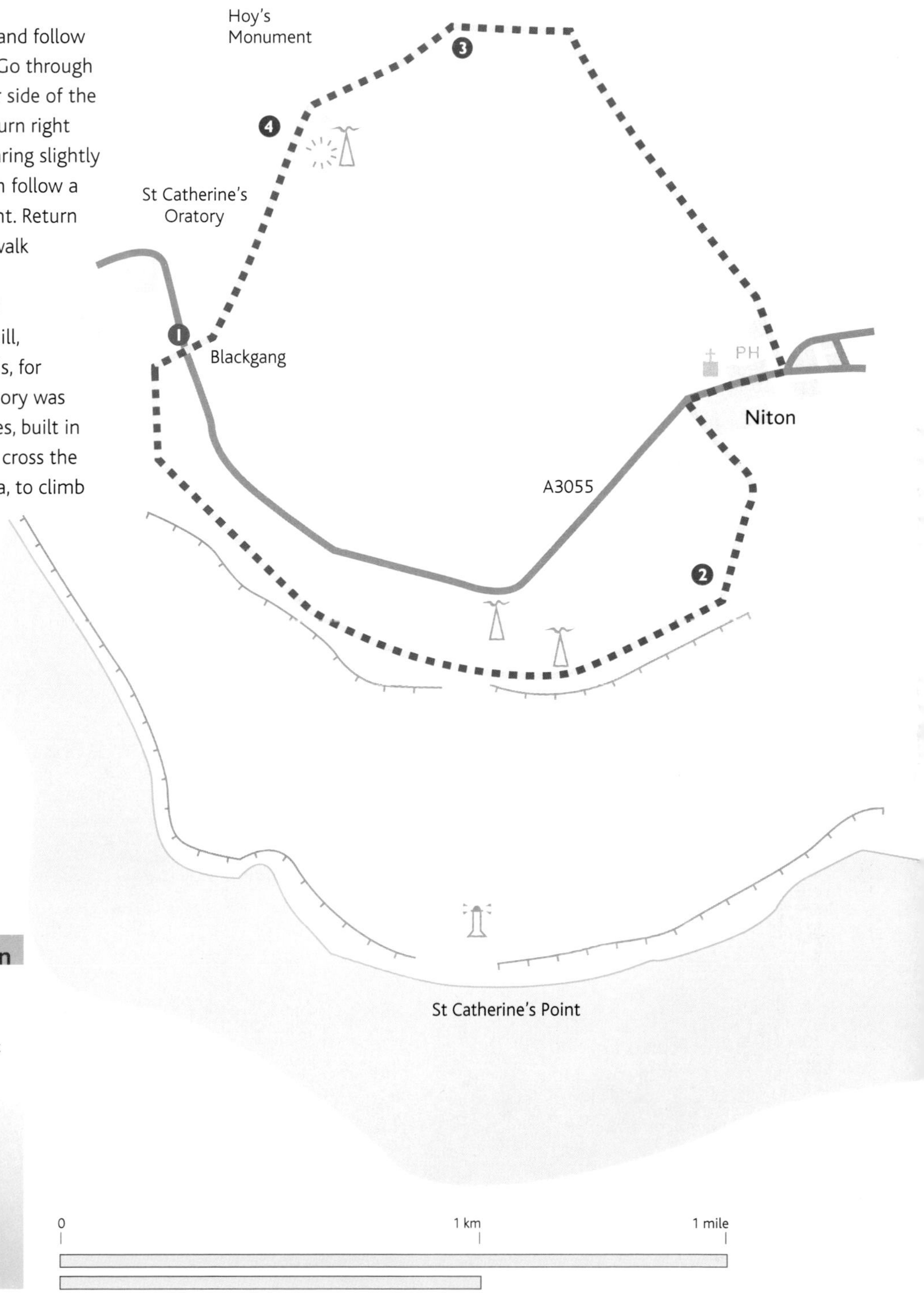

Hoy's Monument

St Catherine's Oratory

Blackgang

Niton

A3055

St Catherine's Point

further information

A Heritage Coast information board in the car park tells you about the area. Points of interest include St Catherine's Lighthouse, which houses the Niton radio station, and Hoy's Monument, which commemorates Czar Alexander I's visit to England and also honours British soldiers who fell during the Crimean War.

0   1 km   1 mile

▲ Map: Explorer 144
▲ Distance: 10 km/6¼ miles
▲ Walk ID: 1348 David Stewart

Difficulty rating

Time

▲ Pub, Church, Great Views

North Oakley and Hannington from White Hill

This circular walk has very little climbing, but really fantastic views nonetheless. The route follows the Wayfarers Walk, then a combination of paths, tracks and small country roads. The last section along the escarpment makes a great finale.

❶ Take the Wayfarers Walk from beside the car park entrance. The path crosses some fields then bears right, down to a road. Turn left on the road, then right on a track past Walkeridge Farm. Go into a field used as a caravan site and walk on down the slope.

❷ Go through a gate and continue ahead along the grassy path until you meet a track. Turn left to walk into North Oakley. Turn left at the road junction, then left again up a driveway, following the footpath sign, and climb a stile. Cross a patch of grass diagonally right to the corner. Cross two more stiles, then head across the field. Bear left at the end. After a short distance bear right across the next field.

❸ Follow the path through the hedge to the road, and turn left into Hannington. Cross the village green and follow the lane right of the churchyard. Follow the footpath on your left, signposted alongside a barn, to a gate onto an open field. Turn right and follow the field edge to the road. Turn right.

❹ Almost immediately, turn left on a signposted footpath. At the corner of the field, turn sharp left up the hill, then bear right by the woods. Follow the path over the hill, down into the valley and up again. At a prominent water tank,

continue straight ahead.

❺ Follow the track when it bends left, climbing a stile to a path around the contour of the hill through woodland. At a fork, turn left, continuing around the hill to reach a field boundary at the radio mast. Drop down to the right a little and follow the path just outside the field below the mast.

❻ Climb a stile signposted to the left and walk straight up the hill. At the top of the field, turn right at a junction of paths and follow the field edge. Cross a stile and bear left slightly. Follow the path down to rejoin the Wayfarers Way and return to the car park.

access information

The White Hill car park is on the B3051 between Overton and Kingsclere, south of the A339.

further information

The Vine in Hannington, a combined pub and restaurant, makes a good stopping point at around the halfway point.

Among the magnificent sights worth visiting on the Wayfarers Walk is the spine-chilling Combe Gibbet at Inkpen Hill.

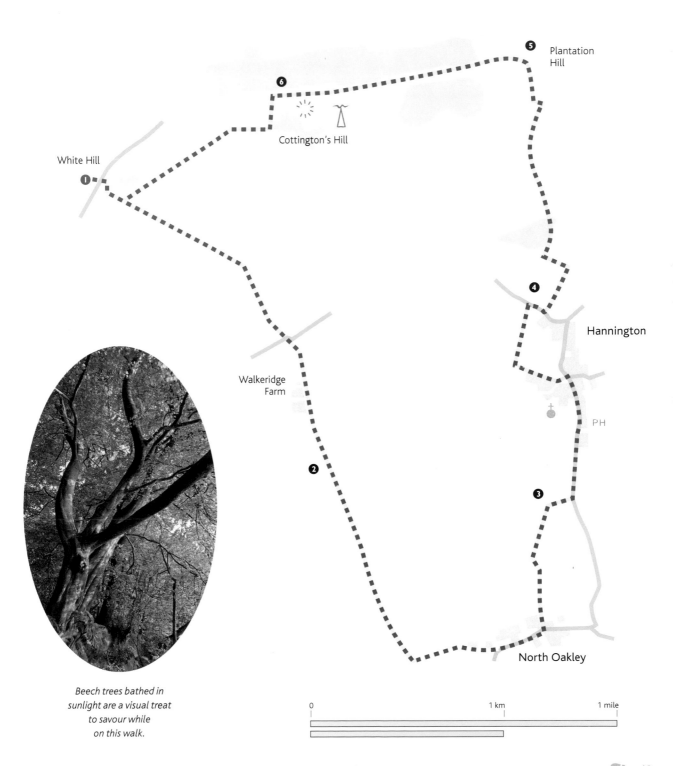

Plantation Hill

White Hill

Cottington's Hill

Hannington

Walkeridge Farm

North Oakley

PH

Beech trees bathed in
sunlight are a visual treat
to savour while
on this walk.

0   1 km   1 mile

▲ Map: Explorer 118
▲ Distance: 10.7 km/6¾ miles
▲ Walk ID: 486 Al Rodger

Difficulty rating

Time

●●●

▲ Hills, Pub, Church, Birds, Great Views

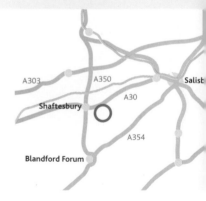

Win Green and Tollard Royal

This peaceful circular walk starts at Win Green Hill, the highest point on Cranborne Chase, with exceptional views. The route follows a tree-lined dry valley to Tollard Royal, then returns on a mostly gradual climb to the main ridgeway.

1 From the car park, walk towards the clump of trees, passing either side of them to reach the ridgeway. Around the first corner, climb a stile over the right-hand fence into the trees and descend the steep hillside on the path slanting right. The path becomes somewhat indistinct, but aim to keep up from the valley bottom until turning right as the side valley comes in from the right.
2 Follow the main track over the rise and down the valley, following the marker posts. (The path passes through a cottage garden but to avoid upsetting the occupants, bypass the cottage on the track.) Where the main track bends right, turn left down to the fence, crossing two stiles and going up through a gate to the track along the left side of the valley.
3 When you meet another track, either walk down into Tollard Royal or head up the track, then turn right and cross a stile to follow a footpath pointer. The path slants left up the hill then crosses fields over the top of the hill.

access information

From the A30 Shaftesbury to Salisbury road, turn right in Ludwell at the signpost to the Larmer Tree Garden. As you climb onto the Chase, look for a signpost Byway to Win Green on the left, and follow the pot-holed road to the car park.

further information

Cranborne Chase was originally a royal hunting ground, popular with King John, and run by the Lord of the Chase. Privately owned from the 1600s to 1830, the Lord of the Chase owned the deer and game which, along with the woods they bred in, were protected. Tolls were charged during fawning and crop damage caused by hunters went uncompensated.

4 Cross a stile beside a gate and follow the path slanting down the hill to the left to join a track in the valley bottom. Go through a gate and climb up the track ahead. At the next fence line, follow the track round to the right and through a gate alongside trees, keeping out of the field.
5 Emerging from the wood, follow the route left off the track, then right into the field, heading for the gap in the trees on the skyline. At the crossroads on the top of the ridge, turn left. When the road begins to drop off the ridge, fork left on the track.
6 At the junction of tracks and road, walk straight on and take the track rising over the hill ahead, meeting the outward route and following the track back to the car park.

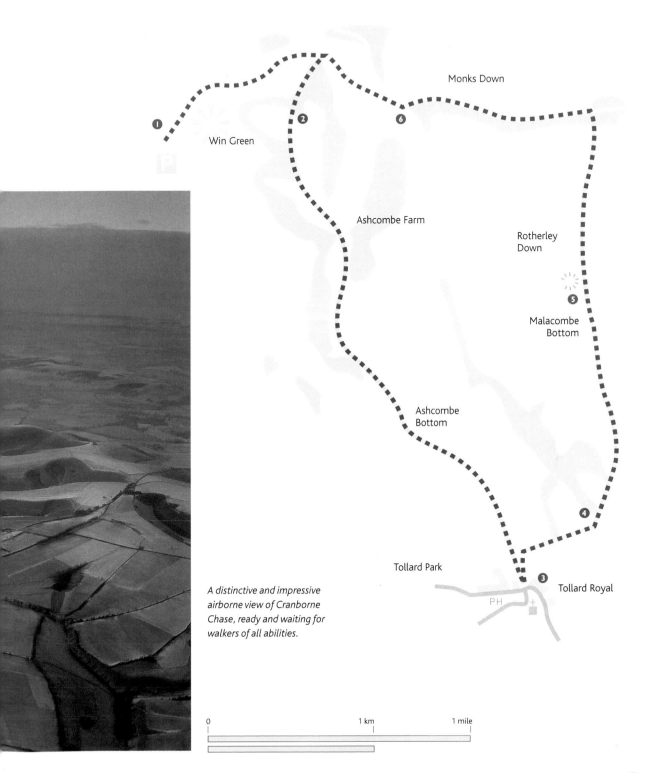

Monks Down

Win Green

Ashcombe Farm

Rotherley
Down

Malacombe
Bottom

Ashcombe
Bottom

Tollard Park

Tollard Royal

*A distinctive and impressive
airborne view of Cranborne
Chase, ready and waiting for
walkers of all abilities.*

0   1 km   1 mile

▲ Map: Explorer 157
▲ Distance: 8.5 km/5¼ miles
▲ Walk ID: 68 David Stewart

Difficulty rating

Time

▲ Pub, Museum, National Trust/NTS, Gift Shop, Restaurant, Great Views

The Sanctuary, West Kennet Long Barrow and Silbury Hill from Avebury

From the Avebury stone circle, this walk goes along the Stone Avenue and up to the Ridgeway with its views of 'hedgehogs' and curious burial mounds. The route then visits The Sanctuary, the West Kennet Long Barrow and Silbury Hill burial ground.

❶ From the car park, follow the signs to Avebury village. At the road, turn right into the ring. Follow the ring round to the left. Cross the main road into the next part of the ring. Bear right and climb up onto the bank. Go down the other side towards a gate. Cross the road into the field. Walk down Stone Avenue between the stones.

❷ At the end of Stone Avenue go through a gate, cross the road, and follow the path opposite. Keeping on the same side of the hedge, cross into the next field. Follow the left-hand field edge slightly uphill to the next field boundary.

❸ Turn right on the track leading towards the 'hedgehogs', a clump of trees on the horizon. Follow the path as it bears left after the hedgehogs, then turn right and follow the Ridgeway down to cross the main road.

❹ Visit The Sanctuary on the right, then follow the path signed 'Byway', directly opposite the end of the Ridgeway. Just before the path turns left and crosses a bridge, turn right and follow the path alongside the river to a road.

A fine view of Avebury village with its ancient stone circle and curious burial mounds.

access information

Avebury lies halfway between Marlborough and Calne, just off the A4. The National Trust provides a free car park just before reaching Avebury village on the A4361. Buses are available from Devizes, Marlborough and Swindon (Wiltshire Bus Line, 0345 090899).

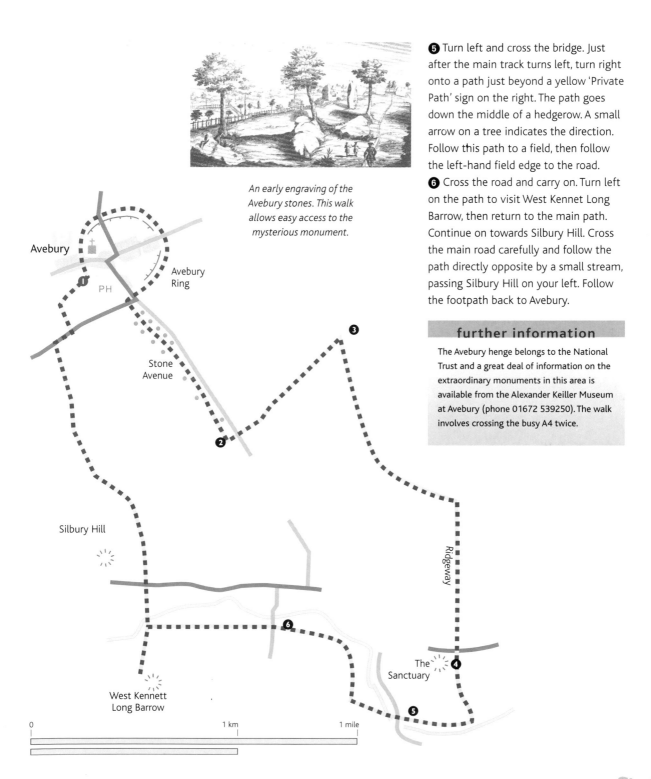

An early engraving of the Avebury stones. This walk allows easy access to the mysterious monument.

Avebury

Avebury Ring

PH

Stone Avenue

Silbury Hill

West Kennett Long Barrow

The Sanctuary

Ridgeway

0   1 km   1 mile

❺ Turn left and cross the bridge. Just after the main track turns left, turn right onto a path just beyond a yellow 'Private Path' sign on the right. The path goes down the middle of a hedgerow. A small arrow on a tree indicates the direction. Follow this path to a field, then follow the left-hand field edge to the road.

❻ Cross the road and carry on. Turn left on the path to visit West Kennet Long Barrow, then return to the main path. Continue on towards Silbury Hill. Cross the main road carefully and follow the path directly opposite by a small stream, passing Silbury Hill on your left. Follow the footpath back to Avebury.

further information

The Avebury henge belongs to the National Trust and a great deal of information on the extraordinary monuments in this area is available from the Alexander Keiller Museum at Avebury (phone 01672 539250). The walk involves crossing the busy A4 twice.

▲ Map: Explorer 135
▲ Distance: 9.5 km/6 miles
▲ Walk ID: 1076 Matthew Mayer

Difficulty rating

Time

▲ Lake, Pub, Toilets, Birds, Food Shop,
Public Transport, Tea Shop, Woodland

Horsted Keynes to Sheffield Park

This walk starts at the Bluebell Railway station at Horsted Keynes. The route passes through this pretty village, then through woods and farmland, following part of the West Sussex Border Path, to Sheffield Park station. Return in style by steam train.

1 From the station, turn left. Follow the road behind the car park. Take the first right turn towards wooden gates. Go through the kissing gates alongside, and down a wooded path. Climb a stile and follow the footpath to another stile. At the road, turn left and cross over. Walk up the drive of Leamlands Barn.

2 Go through the metal gate and turn right. At the field boundary, cross into the next field and follow the path around to the left and over a stile. At a crossroads, follow the footpath straight on. Cross a small bridge, then three more bridges to a track. Turn right, passing a lake.

3 At the crossroads, follow the red arrow across the fields, climbing a stile. At the road, turn right. Go straight across at the junction. Cross the main road in Horsted Keynes. Fork left down Chapel Lane. Cross to Wyatts Lane. Follow the West Sussex Border Path through a small wood and up a hill. Turn left along the Border Path.

4 Turn right along the rough road to a T-junction. Fork left to reach the main road. Turn right, then left towards Kidborough Farm. Fork right at the 'No Horses' sign. Follow the field edge. Go through the wood and cross two fields to a road. Turn right, then left after Town Place. Follow the left-hand field edge. Cross a stile and bridge and turn right.

5 Follow a footpath sign across the railway bridge. Cross the field to a stile. Cross two more stiles to the road. Turn left to a left turning to Bacon Wish. Cross a stile. Follow the main path through the wood.

6 Passing the main path to the right, follow another yellow arrow right, down the slope. Cross a stile and turn left along the field edge, crossing to skirt the next wood. Cross another stile. Turn right across the grass through the wooden gate. Fork left at the road to the main road. Turn left to Sheffield Park station.

further information

The Bluebell Railway uses original steam locomotives to give today's visitors a taste of the Age of Steam. From Sheffield Park, it is possible to return to Horsted Keynes for about £3. If you are planning to travel on the Bluebell Railway, check the timetable by phoning 01825 722370 (24 hours) or visit www.bluebell-railway.co.uk.

A truly spectacular view across a reflective lily pond to the imposing Sheffield Park.

Horsted Keynes Station

Horsted Keynes

PH

Wyatts

West Sussex Border Path

Kidborough Farm

Town Place

PH

Sheffield Park

A rare treat for everyone: the age of steam revisited on the Bluebell Railway that runs from Sheffield Park to Horsted Keynes stations.

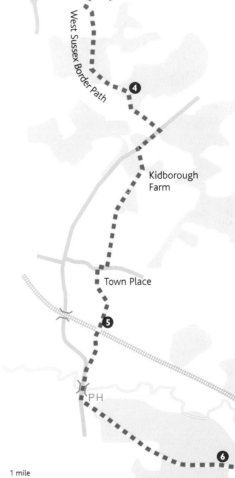

0   1 km   1 mile

▲ Map: Explorer 121
▲ Distance: 8.5 km/5¼ miles
▲ Walk ID: 75 Nicholas Rudd-Jones

Difficulty rating

Time

▲ Hills, Pub, Church, National Trust/NTS, Wildlife, Birds, Great Views, Woodland

The Sussex Downs.

Sutton, Barlavington and South Downs Way

This varied walk climbs to the top of the South Downs, where there are great views of the Downs and the south coast. Much of the walk follows lovely woodland paths.

❶ From the car park, walk up through the gate and alongside the stone wall. Turn right through the gate, climb the stone steps and turn right behind the building. Cross the garden to the kissing gate. Cross the field diagonally left to the far edge. Follow the grassy path straight ahead. At the meadow corner, walk straight ahead though the woods.

❷ Cross a stream and a stile. Turn right towards a gate. Climb a stile and turn left to Barlavington. Turn left along the track. Go through gates into the churchyard and out at the far side. Follow the road round to the left. At the junction, follow the bridleway uphill and into the woods, swinging left. At a small bench, follow the chalky right-hand path. Leave the woods and turn left.

❸ At the crossroads, follow the path uphill across the field. Go through the gate, the woods and another gate, then between fields to more woods. At the next junction, turn right uphill, then immediately left uphill. At the blue waymark, join the track uphill to the left. Keep left, following the National Trust sign to the Bignor Hill car park. Walk downhill past the 'Roman Villa' sign.

❹ Turn left on a steep signposted footpath. Later, join a track to the right then immediately turn left, leaving the woods. Follow the field edge, climb a stile, and cross the fields. Ignore a yellow waymarked stile and swing right along the track into woods. Pass a house on your left and at the road turn left to walk into Bignor.

❺ Go through the gate to the left of the next house and follow the path into woods. Cross a footbridge. Follow the path to another footbridge. Bear right at the footpath sign. Cross a footbridge and a stile. Head for the footpath sign across the meadow then uphill to a stile. Cross the field to Sutton. Follow the path between trees back to the pub.

further information

There is much evidence of the area's long history along this route, which passes several tumuli and a Neolithic camp. At Bignor, there are the remains of a Roman villa. The raised bank crossing the track at Step 3 is Stane Street, a Roman road.

access information

Sutton lies between the A285 Petworth to Chichester road and the A29 Pulborough to Bognor Regis road. Parking is available at the White Horse Pub in Sutton (patrons only, so if you park here it is necessary to patronize at some point).

▲ Map: Explorer 123
▲ Distance: 6.44 km/4 miles
▲ Walk ID: 590 Martin Heaps

Difficulty rating

Time

▲ Sea, Pub, Toilets, National Trust/NTS, Great Views

East Dean Round

This is an easy walk on grassy downland paths and farm tracks. There are wonderful views from the start of the walk over Eastbourne and further east towards Pevensey Marshes and Hastings, and later from Went Hill.

❶ From the bus stop, follow the well-defined grassy path, which starts nearby, towards the sea. When the triangulation point comes into view with the dew pond nearby, bear right towards the road and keep to the right.

❷ Cross the road carefully and go through the gate on the far side. Follow the path, which can get muddy, past Crapham Down and into East Hale Nottom, passing a pumping station. Walk on through the next gate and past a group of farm buildings to join a concrete track at Cornish Farm.

❸ Follow the track round to the left, heading towards Belle Tout, a disused lighthouse now converted to a residential home. When you reach the road, cross over to join the path and turn right towards Birling Gap.

❹ When the road alongside turns almost back on itself to the right, walk on through the car park towards the toilet block, and turn left onto the stony track. Follow the track as it bears right up Went Hill.

❺ Where the path forks left, turn right downhill towards East Dean. The path bears right to a gate, then passes several houses and becomes a narrow road. The road emerges on the village green.

❻ Facing the Tiger Inn, walk to the left and onto the main road. At the road, turn right and then left when you reach Downsview Lane. This track runs parallel to the road through the golf course and back to the start of the walk.

further information

The energetic can access the start point from the town centre along the A259 towards Brighton. The climb up East Dean Hill can be somewhat taxing, but is certainly rewarding for the views.

access information

The start and end point is easily accessible from Eastbourne town centre, with a bus stop only a short distance away.

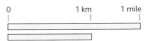

Glimpses of the evocative chalk hills of the South Downs are to be enjoyed on the coastal part of the journey.

▲ Map: Explorer 145

▲ Distance: 12.1 km/7½ miles

▲ Walk ID: 67 Liz and David Fishlock

Difficulty rating

Time

▲ River, Pub, Toilets, Museum, Play Area, Wildlife, Birds

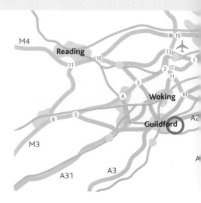

Netley Heath and Shere from Newlands Corner

This walk has two sections. The first follows the North Downs Way for 5 km/3 miles through woodland, while the second crosses open grassland before the final ascent back to the start. If you have time, explore Shere village on the River Tilling Bourne.

❶ From the car park, walk back towards the road, then follow the North Downs Way off to the right, signposted with a blue arrow. Cross the road, then follow the path ahead. At the West Hangar car park, carry on ahead to meet a minor road. Turn right, then fork left on a path leading to a surfaced track. Bear left to a junction of tracks.

❷ Turn left, passing a house and stables. At a crossing track, carry on ahead through the woods, to a junction of tracks by a bench marked Gravelhill Gate. Turn right, leaving the North Downs Way, to pass Colekitchen Farm.

❸ At the top of the hill, follow a bridleway on your right near a white 'Private Drive' sign. Near the top of the hill, soon after a left-hand path, fork left through wooden barriers. Follow the path round to the left and down to cross the main road. Turn left, then right into Queen Street.

❹ Turn right into Gravelpits Lane. At Gravelpits Farmhouse, follow the path to the right of the house. At a crossing track, turn right to Shere. Turn left into the village. Turn right, then left into Lower Street. Follow the road round to the right, crossing a ford.

❺ Turn left on an enclosed footpath beside the Old Rectory wall. Cross the lane and carry on. Go through a kissing gate. Cross the field and walk through the wood. Cross a stile. Follow the left-hand field edge, then walk ahead to a stile. Follow the track to a road. Cross over and follow the right-hand field edge. Cross a stile into woodland. Where the path emerges, cross a driveway. Continue straight ahead.

❻ Cross a stile to the right of Timbercroft and carry on ahead. When you reach cottages, follow a track to the right of the driveway down to a T-junction. Turn right. Follow this main track to turn left at a bridleway sign back to the car park.

further information

The North Downs Way is some 240km/ 150 miles long and travellers have used this ancient track since the Stone Age. To read about the flora and fauna associated with the chalk hills of the North Downs, visit the Countryside Information Centre (open weekends and Bank Holidays) in the car park.

access information

Park at Newlands Corner, which is signposted on the A25 Guildford to Dorking road. If you are travelling by bus or train, start the walk at Step 4 after turning down Queen Street from the main A25. The route crosses the A25 close to the bus stop here, and Gomshall railway station is 5 minutes' walk away (exit the station and walk along the A25 towards Guildford).

This walk passes the exquisite Shere Church in the village of Shere.

The rolling countryside of
the North Downs provides a
beautiful backdrop for this
lovely walk.

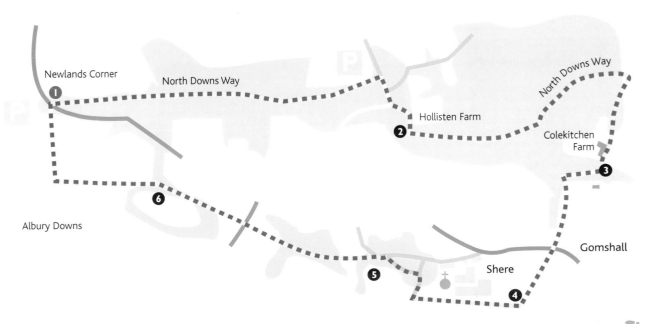

▲ Map: Explorer 124
▲ Distance: 8.5 km/5¼ miles
▲ Walk ID: 206 Jacky Rix-Brown

Difficulty rating

Time

▲ River, Sea, Toilets, Museum, Church, Castle, Wildlife, Birds, Flowers, Great Views

1066 Walk – Battle to Bexhill

This spur of the 1066 Walk from Pevensey to Rye via Battle, takes you from Battle to Bexhill-on-Sea. It starts at Battle Abbey and heads south through rolling hills, the Fore Wood Nature Reserve and the village of Crowhurst on the way to Bexhill.

❶ From the Abbey, walk past the Pilgrim's Rest restaurant. At the track, follow the 1066 walk symbol. When the track divides, fork left to Bexhill, past the wood, over a hill and across a stream. Carry on, crossing a tarmacked track, and climb a stile to follow the path parallel to a road.

❷ Climb the stile and cross the road carefully to Talham Lane opposite. Fork right to Peppering Eye Farm and follow the path straight ahead up the hill. At the junction of paths near a cottage, fork left through the woods, following the 1066 symbol. Turn left downhill with the footpath. Cross the stream into another wood.

❸ Bend right on the main track and follow it through the wood. Just past a pond on the left, fork right to the stile at the edge of the wood. Follow the 1066 symbol across the field, bear left up the hill and continue to the road.

❹ Turn right to Crowhurst. Turn right through the churchyard and out at the bottom gate. Turn right down the hill and follow the road through the village. Where the road bends sharp left, turn right over a stile to follow the footpath beside a stream.

❺ Just past Adam's Farm, follow the 1066 sign to the right. Follow the zigzag path to cross a bridge, then continue across the marshland to climb a stile.

Continue up the valley, then cross a field and the disused railway. Follow the track past Little Worsham Farm. Turn right at the T-junction, then left at another junction to Upper Worsham Farm.

❻ Where the track forks, climb a stile and follow the path, crossing a stream, to reach the A2036. Cross to follow a footpath between gardens to a road. Following the 1066 signs, turn left to the next junction, then right along another road leading to a footpath which crosses the A259 and continues to a road leading to the car park.

access information

Battle lies at the junction of the A271 with the A2100 between Hastings and Hailsham. Bexhill is on the A259. Parking is difficult in Battle, so it is easier to start in the car park in Bexhill, where the walk ends, and catch the no. 328 bus from Town Hall Square to Battle (for information, phone County BusLine 01797 223053). Bexhill is on the railway line between Hastings and Eastbourne, and Battle is on the main Hastings to London line, but not all trains stop there.

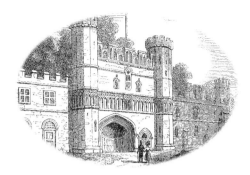

further information

The 1066 walk commemorates the Battle of Hastings, where William the Conqueror famously defeated King Harold on Senlac Hill. There are plenty of places of interest to visit along the walk, including Battle Abbey, the ancient church and centuries-old yew tree in Crowhurst and the museum and ruins of a manor in Bexhill.

Battle Abbey which was built on the site of the defining battle between William the Conqueror and King Harold.

Peaceful now, this is the site of the Battle of Hastings, 1066, near the historic town of Battle in East Sussex.

▲ Map: Explorer 133
▲ Distance: 9.02 km/5¹/₂ miles
▲ Walk ID: 1289 Ray Clarke

Difficulty rating

Time

▲ Toilets, Wildlife, Flowers, Great Views, Café

Butser Hill Trail

This is a satisfying walk, which gets the heart pumping as you climb the hill. Look for birds, rabbits, sheep, the occasional fox, flowers and fine views of the South Downs. On a clear day, you can see as far as the Isle of Wight.

1 From the car park, return to the entrance and walk under the bridge beneath the main road.

2 After a short distance, cross the car park access road at the fingerpost sign and follow the blue horseshoe signs. Go through a gate and follow the path up the hill, passing between two belts of woodland and heading roughly in the direction of the radio mast. Go through a gate halfway up.

3 Carry on through another gate and bear round to the left towards a small circular building that resembles an Iron Age house. Follow the road past the building and out of the car park, passing the pay-and-display meter. After a short distance, turn right to follow a broad track down the hill. Where the track forks at Butser Hill, bear left, passing woodland on your right. The track bears right and left, passing Leythe House on the right to reach a lane.

4 Turn right along the lane. When you reach a crossroads with the Ramsdean road signposted to the left, follow the track to the right.

5 After a short distance, climb a stile on the left and follow the track, passing first through woodland then climbing up the spine of the hill, heading just to the right of the radio mast. Continue along the path until you meet the road back to the car park.

6 Cross straight over the road, then turn left and retrace your steps through the gate and back down the hill to the first gate. Return to the car park.

This breathtaking view across the ancient countryside of Hampshire is from Butser Hill near Petersfield.

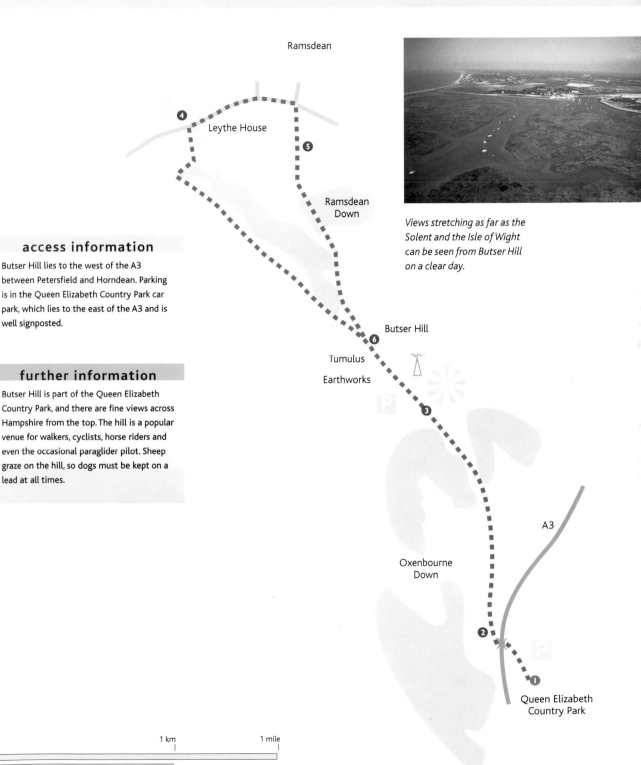

Ramsdean

Leythe House

Ramsdean
Down

*Views stretching as far as the
Solent and the Isle of Wight
can be seen from Butser Hill
on a clear day.*

access information

Butser Hill lies to the west of the A3
between Petersfield and Horndean. Parking
is in the Queen Elizabeth Country Park car
park, which lies to the east of the A3 and is
well signposted.

further information

Butser Hill is part of the Queen Elizabeth
Country Park, and there are fine views across
Hampshire from the top. The hill is a popular
venue for walkers, cyclists, horse riders and
even the occasional paraglider pilot. Sheep
graze on the hill, so dogs must be kept on a
lead at all times.

Butser Hill

Tumulus

Earthworks

A3

Oxenbourne
Down

Queen Elizabeth
Country Park

0   1 km   1 mile

▲ Map: Explorer 192
▲ Distance: 8.86 km/5½ miles
▲ Walk ID: 1122 Tony Brotherton

Difficulty rating

Time

▲ Hills, Lake, Pub, Toilets, Play Area, Church, Stately Home, Wildlife, Birds, Flowers, Great Views, Butterflies, Food Shop

Around Woburn

This is a gentle circular walk from the village of Woburn, crossing the Bedford Estate with its deer park, then looping around through farmland on the Greensand Ridge Walk to return across the park with a fine view of the glorious Woburn Abbey.

❶ From the car park, turn right down Park Street. Take the signposted footpath immediately right after the lodge. Follow the drive through Park Farm and over staggered cross-paths to walk to the left of the water. Walk diagonally left across the parkland to a small rise. At the vehicle entrance to Woburn, walk downhill to the estate gates.

❷ Fork right towards Milton Bryan. At Hills End Cottages, turn left on the footpath. Climb the stile and cross the field to an orange-topped waymark post. Keep ahead, and at the next post turn right. Cross a footbridge and cross the next field straight ahead. Cross a stile to a gravel drive leading to a lane.

❸ Turn left past Helford House, then turn right on a footpath. Follow the left-hand field edge to a hedged path. Follow the right-hand hedge in the next field. After the next waymark post, turn right and follow the Greensand Ridge Walk to the road at Church End, Eversholt.

❹ Walk through the village. At the T-junction, turn right. Just before the road bends, turn right through a gate and follow the Greensand Ridge Walk sign diagonally across the field. Cross a stream at a double stile to reach cross-paths and a signpost, with the lake on your right.

❺ Follow the Greensand Ridge Walk, crossing the stream again, to a stile. Follow the path across a field and through trees, then uphill through a plantation. The path continues uphill and into the deer park, then downhill to a path junction after the Abbey entrance.

❻ Keep ahead. At the crossing track, continue ahead on a narrow causeway between ponds and cross the parkland, following occasional small posts. Go through a gate at the corner of the woods to a fenced path to the road ahead. Turn right to Woburn village, then right into Park Street to the car park.

further information

Woburn Abbey, now a famous stately home occupied by the Duke and Duchess of Bedfordshire, is one of several great residences that were created after Henry VIII's Dissolution of the Monasteries in the late 1530s, either being converted from the original monastic buildings or built on former monastic sites.

access information

Woburn lies on the A4012 which loops east of Leighton Buzzard to join the A5130 to Milton Keynes. There is free parking in the village car park in Park Street.

When walking through Woburn Park, look out for herds of deer or an encounter with the occasional shy lone animal.

About halfway round the walk, the route passes Church End, Eversholt, before striking out towards the Greensand Ridge Walk.

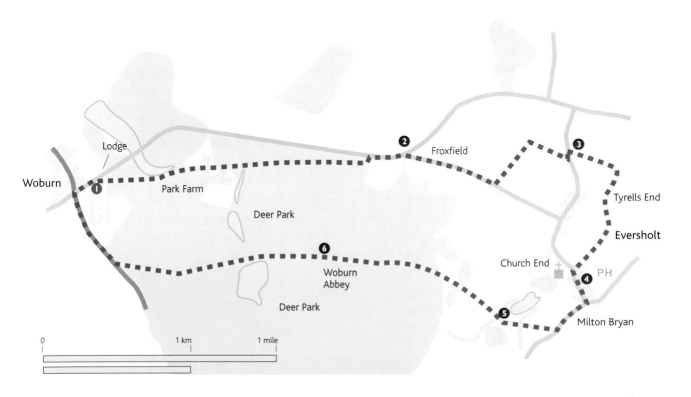

▲ Map: Explorer 180
▲ Distance: 8.45 km/5¼ miles
▲ Walk ID: 1234 Ron and Jenny Glynn

Difficulty rating

Time

▲ Lake, Church, Stately Home, Wildlife, Birds, Flowers, Great Views, Butterflies, Woodland

Wotton Underwood from Ludgershall

This gentle walk begins in Ludgershall and wanders through Buckinghamshire on a mixture of footpaths, bridleways and quiet country roads. The route passes through the beautiful parkland surrounding the magnificent Wotton House.

1 Take the minor road, just before the church at Peartree Farm, signed to Wotton, and walk along to the junction. Walk over to the narrow path at Wotton End, and follow the hedge line to cross a brook. Fork right over common ground to an opening.

2 Walk past the stile on the left at a junction of paths, and follow the left-hand hedge in ridge and furrow meadowland. Climb a stile and cross the next two fields, with woodland over to the left. Cross a double stile and footbridge. Turn right on a bridleway, with the hedge on your right. Go through a walkers' gate and then another gate.

3 Cross the road and another stile. Cross a large field, with farm buildings on your right, gradually climbing uphill. Head slightly right over two stiles. Climb a stile in the corner of the field to a hard track. Walk over and cross the stile to the left of the white gate to Middle Farm. Follow the field edge until you reach a metal kissing gate.

4 Turn right through a wooden gate and pass the back of a farmhouse to a hard path, passing through a wild flower meadow and crossing a miniature railway track. Pass a redbrick house, then turn right through a gate to walk by Wotton House. The path runs downhill.

5 Walk ahead over a large green to join the road, and follow it along between trees and hedgerows. Turn right past Lawn Farm. Just before the railway, fork right towards Ludgershall and Kingswood on a narrow road through woodland.

6 At the junction at the end of the woodland, follow the lane ahead to Ludgershall. Turn left into Church Lane, and retrace your steps to the start.

After Middle Farm the walk passes the grandiose Wotton House, in Wotton Underwood, seen here with the 'ha ha' in the foreground.

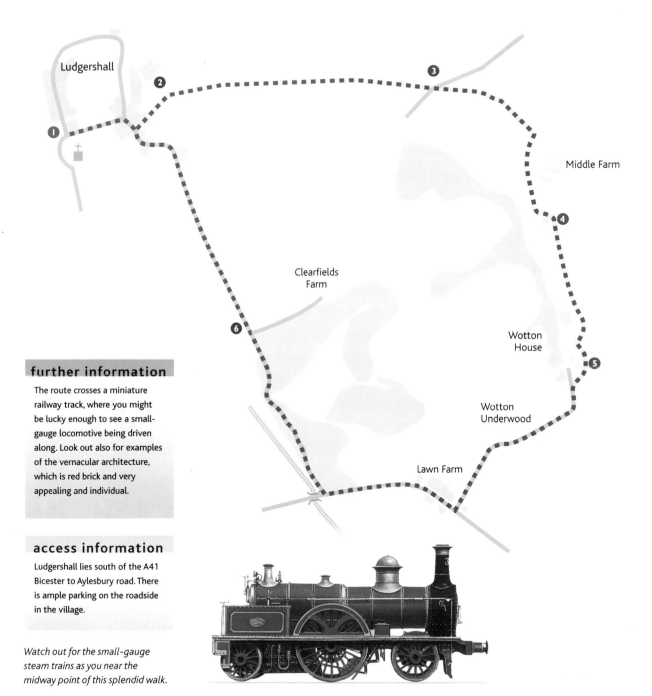

Ludgershall

Middle Farm

Clearfields
Farm

Wotton
House

Wotton
Underwood

Lawn Farm

further information

The route crosses a miniature
railway track, where you might
be lucky enough to see a small-
gauge locomotive being driven
along. Look out also for examples
of the vernacular architecture,
which is red brick and very
appealing and individual.

access information

Ludgershall lies south of the A41
Bicester to Aylesbury road. There
is ample parking on the roadside
in the village.

*Watch out for the small-gauge
steam trains as you near the
midway point of this splendid walk.*

0   1 km   1 mile

▲ Map: Explorer 181
▲ Distance: 7.25 km/4½ miles
▲ Walk ID: 212 Liz and David Fishlock

Difficulty rating

Time

▲ Pub, Birds, Flowers, Great Views

Windmill Walk from Parslows Hillock

further information

The windmill in Lacey Green has been restored by the Chiltern Society, and is open to the public on Sunday afternoons between May and September from 2.30 to 5.30 p.m. Access to the windmill is along a path just before the Whip Inn, which you pass at Step 3.

This is a flat, open walk with just one steep climb in the final stages. The Pink and Lily pub at the start was a favourite haunt of the World War I poet, Rupert Brooke. Allow extra time to visit the windmill at Lacey Green, believed to date from 1650.

❶ Walk past the pub and down Lily Bottom Lane to Hillock Cottages. Turn right up the Chiltern Way, then climb a right-hand stile and cross the field diagonally left. Cross the stile and the field towards a gate. Climb another stile and follow the fenced path, ignoring a farm track and a stile on your right.

❷ Climb the next stile and cross the field diagonally right. Climb another stile. At the hedgerow corner, follow the right-hand field edge. Cross another stile and follow the right-hand field edge. Cross a stile and a field to the main road. Turn right, then right into Pink Road.

❸ Cross the road at Widmer Farm and climb the stile. Cross the field. Before the power line pole, climb a stile on your right. Turn left, then cross another stile on your right and turn left. Go under the power lines and cross another stile. Follow the left-hand field edge.

❹ Cross the corner stile and turn right. Cross a stile and walk down to the road. Turn right. Cross to Wardrobes Lane. Cross the stile and the field corner. Cross a stile, and bear diagonally left. Cross a stile and follow the right-hand field edge. Carry on, crossing the farm drive.

❺ Where the field edge bears right, go straight ahead. At the rise, carry on across two stiles, a field and a stile. Go under the power lines, then follow the left-hand field edge. Just before the wood on your left, turn right across the field. Cross a stile. Turn left along the lane, then right at the road.

❻ At the right bend, turn left over a stile. Walk to another stile. Follow the left-hand field edge to a stile into the wood. Follow the steep path up through the wood, then turn right on a crossing track. Exit through a gate. Turn left along the driveway, then right at the road to the start.

The fascinating windmill at Lacey Green.

access information

From the A4010 Aylesbury to High Wycombe Road, turn into a road called Woodhay, about 750 m/820 yards from the southern outskirts of Princes Risborough (on your right if you are heading towards Princes Risborough, or left if you are leaving Princes Risborough). Follow the road to the crossroads at the Whip Inn, then turn left into Pink Road. Park in the lay-by on the left, just before the Pink & Lily pub.

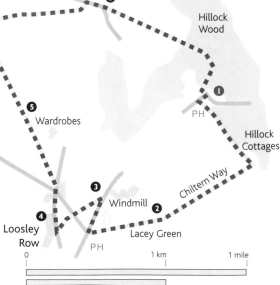

▲ Map: Explorer 192

▲ Distance: 5 km/3 miles

▲ Walk ID: 237 Gill Perkins

Difficulty rating

Time

▲ Hills, Pub, Church, Wildlife, Birds, Great Views

A breathtaking viewpoint.

Quainton Hill

Although fairly short, this circular walk is very rewarding, beginning in the unspoilt village of Quainton, then climbing to the top of Quainton Hill for panoramic views of the Chilterns, the Cotswolds and north Buckinghamshire.

❶ From the entrance to St Mary's Church, walk downhill, with the church on your right, for a short distance to cross two stiles into a field. Walk straight ahead to the next stile in the hedge. The footpath is marked Matthew's Way and Swan's Way.

❷ Climb the stile and cross to the gate in the hedge. Go through the gate and follow the track up the hill towards a telecommunications mast, going through another gate halfway up.

❸ From the top of the hill, with the mast on your right, go through a gate straight ahead and follow the path downhill. Go through another gate and immediately turn left. Continue ahead to climb a stile. Walk through some rough land for a short distance, then cross another stile onto open rolling hills.

❹ Walk across the hills, following the grassy track which runs parallel to the hedge on your left. Climb another stile

access information

Quainton lies north of the A41 between Aylesbury and Bicester. Car parking is available either in Church Street by the almshouses, or anywhere around the church. Trains between Aylesbury and London run frequently. Bus nos. 16, 17 and 18 run from Aylesbury to Quainton every day except Sunday (for information, go to www.pindar.co.uk/bucks/tt/ayndx.htm).

at a junction of paths, and continue ahead on the track. As you walk over the hills, you see Quainton Windmill and the village ahead of you.

❺ When you reach a stile next to a gate, climb the stile. If you like, climb the hill to enjoy the views, then walk back down to continue. Turn left to follow the path round the base of the hill and towards the village rooftops, with the windmill on your left, to a kissing gate.

❻ Cross the sleeper bridge through the gate and pass down a narrow track between two houses to the village. Turn left on Lower Street and walk towards the village green. Walk along the top of the village green, then continue walking down Church Street to return to your car.

further information

Quainton Windmill, built around 1830 with bricks made on the site, is 20 m/60 ft high and has six floors. It is occasionally open to the public (for information, phone 01296 675348 or 01296 675224). St Mary's Church in Quainton contains monuments to various famous people. The market cross at the top of the green dates from the 15th century.

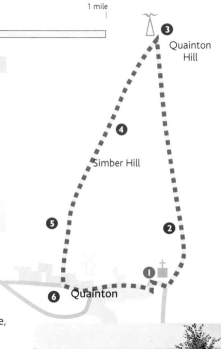

A spectacular reward for the short climb to the top of Quainton Hill – the Chilterns in all their glory.

Index

acknowledgements

The publishers wish to thank the following for the use of pictures: TONY BROTHERTON: pps. 10, 59; CAMERON COLLECTION: pps. 17, 21; COLLECTIONS: pps. 12 David Davies, 15 Jill Swainson, 18/9, 22T, 24, 28 Robert Deane, 30 David M Hughes, 34, 38 Robert Hales Mann, 39 Robert Estall, 42 Robin Weaver, 53 Robert Pilgrim, 54 Philip Craven, 56 + 60 Robert Pilgrim, 62 David Davies, 63T + 63B David Martyn Hughes; CORBIS: pps. 9 Michael Nicholson, 16 John Heseltine, 20 Adam Woolfitt, 22B John Heseltine, 32/3 Robert Estall. 35, 36, 40 John Farmar/Cordaiy Photo Library Ltd., 44/5 Angelo Hornak, 46 Yann Arthus-Bertrand, 48 Roger Antrobus, 49 WA.Sharman/Milepost92½, 57 John Farmar/Ecoscene; GRAHAM HOLLIER: p.13; HUTCHISON PICTURE LIBRARY: pps.26, 50, 52; OLIVER O'BRIEN: pps. 25, 27; DAVID L WHITE: p. 41